# The Greatest American Presidents

*including a Short Course on all the Presidents and Political Parties*

Robert Tata

authorHOUSE®

AuthorHouse™
1663 Liberty Drive
Bloomington, IN 47403
www.authorhouse.com
Phone: 1-800-839-8640

Published by AuthorHouse 4/22/2013

ISBN: 978-1-4817-2268-1 (sc)
ISBN: 978-1-4817-2267-4 (hc)
ISBN: 978-1-4817-2269-8 (e)

Library of Congress Control Number: 2013903824

USA map courtesy of MapsForDesign.com,

Images by my daughter Judy.

# Overview

This book is written by a licensed Professional Engineer who has taken an interest in the history of the United States Presidents and political parties. Since the author is not a political scholar, it is more of an "average citizen" approach to the subject matter as opposed to what might be written by political historians.

The author has named what he believes are the greatest presidents of all time focusing on the nature and magnitude of their achievements. There is also a second list of presidents who are described as being "honorable mention". This is not to say that the presidents not making either list have not been able administrators as millions of knowledgeable U.S. citizens voted them in office. All the American presidents have been, for the most part, very capable and honorable chief executives who have served their country well.

At the beginning of this publication, is a detailed chart listing all fifty-seven U.S. presidential elections, complete with winners, losers, dates, and political parties. Following are short profiles of the presidents that are honored; short summaries of all five major political parties; and, short factual summaries of all 44 presidents. In this last section, for some of the early occupants of the White House, the author has selected a modern day president who best exemplifies his earlier counterpart.

# The Presidents* & The Political Parties

| Years | | Federalist | Dem-Repub | Democrat | Whig Party | Republican |
|---|---|---|---|---|---|---|
| 1788-1792 | Washington* | | | | | |
| 1792-1796 | Washington* | | | | | |
| 1796-1800 | | Adams* | Jefferson | | | |
| 1800-1804 | | Adams | Jefferson* | | | |
| 1804-1808 | | Pinckney | Jefferson* | | | |
| 1808-1812 | | Pinckney | Madison* | | | |
| 1812-1816 | | Clinton | Madison* | | | |
| 1816-1820 | | King | Monroe* | | | |
| 1820-1824 | | | Monroe* | | | |
| 1824-1828 | | | AdamsJQ* | | | |
| 1828-1832 | | | AdamsJQ | Jackson* | | |
| 1832-1836 | | | Clay | Jackson* | | |
| 1836-1840 | | | | Van Buren* | Harrison | |
| 1840-1844 | | | | Van Buren | Harrison*/ Tyler* | |

| | | | | | |
|---|---|---|---|---|---|
| 1844-1848 | | | | Polk* | Clay |
| 1848-1852 | | | | Cass | Taylor*/Fillmore* |
| 1852-1856 | | | | Pierce* | Scott |
| 1856-1860 | | | | Buchanan* | | Fremont |
| 1860-1864 | | | | Breckenridge | | Lincoln* |
| 1864-1868 | | | | McClellan | | Lincoln*/Johnson* |
| 1868-1872 | | | | Seymour | | Grant* |
| 1872-1876 | | | | Greeley | | Grant* |
| 1876-1880 | | | | Tilden | | Hayes* |
| 1880-1884 | | | | Hancock | | Garfield*/Arthur* |
| 1884-1888 | | | | Cleveland* | | Blaine |
| 1888-1892 | | | | Cleveland | | Harrison* |
| 1892-1896 | | | | Cleveland* | | Harrison |
| 1896-1900 | | | | Bryan | | McKinley* |
| 1900-1904 | | | | Bryan | | McKinley*/RooseveltT* |
| 1904-1908 | | | | Parker | | RooseveltT* |
| 1908-1912 | | | | Bryan | | Taft* |
| 1912-1916 | | | | Wilson* | | Taft/RooseveltT |
| 1916-1920 | | | | Wilson* | | Hughes |
| 1920-1924 | | | | Cox | | Harding*/Coolidge* |
| 1924-1928 | | | | Davis | | Coolidge* |
| 1928-1932 | | | | Smith | | Hoover* |
| 1932-1936 | | | | RooseveltFD* | | Hoover |

| 1936-1940 | | | | RooseveltFD* | | Landon |
|---|---|---|---|---|---|---|
| 1940-1944 | | | | RooseveltFD* | | Willkie |
| 1944-1948 | | | | RooseveltFD*/Truman* | | Dewey |
| 1948-1952 | | | | Truman* | | Dewey |
| 1952-1956 | | | | Stevenson | | Eisenhower* |
| 1956-1960 | | | | Stevenson | | Eisenhower* |
| 1960-1964 | | | | Kennedy*/Johnson* | | Nixon |
| 1964-1968 | | | | Johnson* | | Goldwater |
| 1968-1972 | | | | Humphrey | | Nixon* |
| 1972-1976 | | | | McGovern | | Nixon*/Ford* |
| 1976-1980 | | | | Carter* | | Ford |
| 1980-1984 | | | | Carter | | Reagan* |
| 1984-1988 | | | | Mondale | | Reagan* |
| 1988-1992 | | | | Dukakis | | BushHW* |
| 1992-1996 | | | | Clinton* | | BushHW |
| 1996-2000 | | | | Clinton* | | Dole |
| 2000-2004 | | | | Gore | | BushW* |
| 2004-2008 | | | | Kerry | | Bush W* |
| 2008-2012 | | | | Obama* | | McCain |
| 2012-2016 | | | | Obama* | | Romney |

# The Eight Greatest Presidents

There have been 57 presidential elections held in the United States and 44 presidents. One president, Franklin Delano Roosevelt, was elected to four terms, more than any other person. Since then, a law has been passed limiting presidents to two terms. Sixteen presidents have been elected to two terms. They are Washington, Jefferson, Madison, Monroe, Jackson, Lincoln, Grant, Cleveland, McKinley, Wilson, Eisenhower, Nixon, Reagan, Clinton, Bush, and Obama. Grover Cleveland was the only president to be elected to two non-consecutive terms; therefore, he is counted as president twice.

The following evaluation of the eight greatest presidents is based on the author's opinion only and is not intended to reflect the view of any other person:

**Frank Delano Roosevelt, 32$^{nd}$ President**: No other man has had to work so diligently, for so long, under such severe troublesome times than Franklin Delano Roosevelt. He did this wearing leg braces throughout his presidency as he contacted polio earlier in his life. He is considered by the author as the greatest president to have ever served this country. FDR was the 32$^{nd}$ president and the only one to serve over two terms. The people loved him so dearly that he was elected to four consecutive terms. FDR beat all four of his Republican opponents with massive electoral vote count margins. FDR served during the Great Depression; during Japan's attack on Pearl Harbor; and, during Germany's attack on Poland prompting World War II. His predecessor, Herbert Hoover, tried to take the country out of the Great Depression but was unsuccessful. Roosevelt pushed through Congress massive relief programs to help end the depression. He led the United States victoriously through the war on Japan in Asia and through the war on the Axis in Europe. He dealt successfully with more severe internal and external conflict than any other president; and, he did it all while suffering from a crippling physical impairment.

**George Washington, 1st President**: George Washington is believed to be a close second behind FDR as the greatest of all United States Presidents. Among other things, George Washington was a man who loved his country and commanded respect from those around him. He received all of the most important titles of his day; he was the Commander in Chief of the Army that beat the British in the Revolutionary War; he was the president of the convention that wrote the American Constitution; and, he was the first president of the United States receiving all the electoral votes for two full terms. While he was president, he settled differences with England despite his deeply divided cabinet over the treatment of that country following the Revolutionary War. Thomas Jefferson, Washington's Secretary of State, despite having strong political differences with Washington, said of him; "Never did nature and fortune combine more perfectly to make a man great."

**Abraham Lincoln, 16ᵗʰ President**: Rated right under George Washington is Abraham Lincoln who has to be considered one of the greatest of all American presidents. Lincoln, like Washington, was a self-made man receiving no formal education. Lincoln was famous for his writing, his speeches, and his debating ability. He was elected the 16th president when, after sixteen years of congressional bickering failed to settle the slavery issue, war broke out between the North and the South. Lincoln's firm belief that "a house divided against itself cannot stand" gave him the conviction to lead the nation through the lengthy Civil War. All efforts by great American statesmen to avoid war had failed and Lincoln was brave enough to take a stand in settling the issue. The war lasted from 1861 to 1865 with one million U.S. casualties, more than any other conflict. Lincoln's "Gettysburg Address" given during the dedication of the Soldiers National Cemetery in Gettysburg,

Pennsylvania, the site of one of the most famous of all Civil War battles, is considered a literary masterpiece.

**Thomas Jefferson, 3ʳᵈ President**: Next in line of great American presidents is Thomas Jefferson. Jefferson was the third president and the second to serve two terms. Jefferson was active in early American politics. He was a fervent believer in the rights of citizens under the Constitution. He wrote the Declaration of Independence and was one of the people that sponsored the first 10 amendments to the Constitution granting civil liberties to all. He was the leader of the second United States political party, the Democratic-Republican Party. Jefferson was Washington's Secretary of State and Minister to France. His friendly relationship with France helped enact the "Louisiana Purchase". This land stretched from the Mississippi River to the Rocky Mountains, doubling the size of the United States.

**Ronald Reagan, 40ᵗʰ President**: The next man to be recognized as being great and one of the 16 of 44 that served two terms is 40ᵗʰ President Ronald Reagan. He is also one of a few presidents that switched political parties. He switched from the Democrat to the Republican Party before being elected president. Reagan's greatest achievement was a monumental one in which he brought down the Soviet Empire. The U.S. and the U.S.S.R. were cold war enemies since World War II ended in 1945. Each country had stockpiled thousands of nuclear weapons and had developed long range missiles. The missiles had the capability of delivering nuclear weapons anywhere on the globe possibly leading to the destruction of the entire planet. Reagan stood firm in discussions with Russian premier Mikhail Gorbachev and won him over ending the Cold War. Millions of people from the old Soviet Empire were set free. Reagan also stood firm by firing 11,345 Air Traffic Controllers who bypassed the law by going on strike. Reagan lowered individual taxes across the board to help the country out of recession. Reagan's achievement in ending the threat of global nuclear war between the United States and the Soviet Union is considered to be one of the greatest in the history of this country. The world became much more of a peaceful place thanks to Ronald Reagan.

**Dwight David Eisenhower, 34ᵗʰ President**: The president with the most distinguished military career is thought to be Dwight Eisenhower. He graduated from West Point and became an aide to General Douglas MacArthur. He commanded the invasion of North Africa, Sicily, Italy, and Normandy which brought about Germany's surrender and the end of World War II in 1945.

As a two-term president, Eisenhower worked to improve the nation's road network establishing the interstate system of highways. His philosophy was to give more power back to the states. Under him, the United States took the lead in organizing eight nations known as SEATO to resist communism in Southeast Asia. He signed the bill organizing NASA to coordinate U.S. space effort to overtake the Soviets in rocket science during the Cold War. He broke off relations with Cuba after Castro seized United States property. Eisenhower became a very effective leader as president based on the experience he gained as a great military commander. In general, people loved Eisenhower as evidenced by the two easy victories he won over Democratic rivals.

**James Monroe, 5ᵗʰ President**: Not many presidents achieved in office James Monroe's accomplishments. He was the 5ᵗʰ president of the United States and one of the sixteen that served two terms. Following Thomas Jefferson and James Madison, he was the third consecutive Democratic-Republican from Virginia to serve as president.

While in office, the Missouri Compromise was passed temporarily settling the slavery issue; the Monroe Doctrine warned European nations not to interfere with the countries in the Western Hemisphere; the United States purchased Florida from Spain; the boundary between the United States and Canada was established with Great Britain; and, Russia and Spain gave up claims to Oregon. James Monroe is one of the greatest and one of the most underrated of all United States presidents.

**Andrew Jackson, 7ᵗʰ President**: Not many men who were elected to the presidency exhibited as much strength and determination as seventh president Andrew Jackson. He grew up a fighting man. He volunteered his services to the United States Army and won historic battles in the War if 1812 over the British in Alabama and New Orleans. He wasn't pleased with the Democratic-Republican Party and started today's Democrat Party winning two consecutive elections over his old Democrat-Republican rivals. Jackson meant every word uttered in his inaugural address; "The Federal Constitution must be obeyed; states' rights preserved; our national debt paid; direct taxes and loans avoided; and the Federal Union preserved". He paid off the national debt; and, when France failed to make restitution for damages to American shipping, he initiated a military buildup and forced them to make back payments with interest. If every other president had heeded his words, one might think that the United States would be an entirely different country today.

# Great Presidents Honorable Mention

**John Adams, 2ⁿᵈ President**: One of the leaders in the fight for independence for the colonies from England was John Adams. He was a member of the committee that wrote the Declaration of Independence. He was George Washington's Vice-President both terms and he was Washington's successor to the presidency. As president, he signed a peace treaty with France ending attacks on American shipping.

**James Madison, 4ᵗʰ President**: "The Father of the Constitution" is the name given to James Madison as it was written according to his plan. Madison was a two term president during the War of 1812 which the Americans won over Great Britain.

**James K. Polk, 11ᵗʰ President**: Four goals were set by James K. Polk in his presidency and he was to achieve them all. He reduced tariffs. He created the forerunner of the Federal Reserve System. He signed a treaty with Great Britain establishing the border between the Oregon Territory and Canada. He went to war with Mexico and claimed the land now making up seven southwestern states.

**Theodore Roosevelt, 26ᵗʰ President**: No president has enjoyed the office as much as Theodore Roosevelt. He broke up big corporations, built up the Navy, and is responsible for building the Panama Canal.

**Woodrow Wilson, 28ᵗʰ President**: The list of accomplishments for Woodrow Wilson is impressive. He lowered tariffs. He created the

Federal Reserve System, the Federal Trade Commission, and the 8 hour work week.

**Harry S. Truman, 33rd President**: The president presiding over the country during the end of World War II, the beginning of the Cold War with the U.S.S.R., and the Korean War was Harry S. Truman. He made all the tough decisions to end World War II and he fought to combat the expansion of the U.S.S.R. into Western Europe.

**John F. Kennedy, 35th President**: The chief claim to fame for John F. Kennedy is forcing the Russians to turn back their ships loaded with missiles bound for Cuba for possible use against the United States. This act was the start of the fall of Nikita Khrushchev and the U.S.S.R.

**Richard M. Nixon, 37th President**: One of the most controversial presidents is Richard M. Nixon because of the Watergate affair; however, his accomplishments include removing troops from Vietnam; forming the EPA; warming relations with China and Russia; and limiting nuclear weapons.

**George H.W. Bush, 41st President**: Another controversial president is George H.W. Bush as he signed a bill to raise taxes after he vowed against doing it; however, he sent troops to Panama to dethrone the dictator who had become an enemy of the United States; he met with Mikhail Gorbachev and reduced nuclear weapons by 35%; he sent troops to stop the invasion of oil rich Kuwait by Saddam Hussein; and, he started the negotiations that resulted in the North American Free Trade Agreement.

**Barack Obama, 44th President**: The jury is still out on Barack Obama as whether or not he can be classified as great and not just honorable mention. In his first term, he signed legislation to reform health care and to stimulate the economy; two programs that time will tell whether they are great. He ordered the operation that led to the death of long time terrorist leader, Osama bin Laden. The success of his second term in dealing with the country's enormous debt and weak economy will be a major factor in determining his greatness.

# The Political Parties, 1796-2012

There have been 5 major political parties taken part in the 57 elections held in the United States. They are as follows:

**Federalist Party, 1796-1816, (1 of 6 elections won (17%)**: The first political party organized was the Federalist Party. It was formed during Washington's term of office. George Washington did not belong to a political party; although, it is thought that if he had to choose, he would have been a Federalist. The Federalist Party was led by Alexander Hamilton, Washington's Secretary of the Treasury. Hamilton believed in a strong central government, a central bank, a conservative fiscal policy, business, and friendly relations with Great Britain. Federalist Party member John Adams, Washington's Vice-President, won the first presidential election following Washington's two terms. The Federalist Party dissolved after losing the next five elections to Democratic-Republican candidates. The Federalists are thought to be more like today's Republican Party than today's Democratic Party. (See preceding table.)

**Democratic-Republican Party, 1796-1832, (7 of 10 won (70%)**: The second political party to be organized was the Democratic-Republican Party. It was originally called the Republican Party but historians changed the name because it helps to distinguish it from today's party of the same name. It came into being just after the founding of the Federalist Party as it was formed to challenge the Federalists. Both parties were organized during Washington's term in office. The Democratic-

Republican Party was led by Thomas Jefferson, Washington's Secretary of State. Jefferson believed in states' rights, individual liberties, and that the Constitution should be interpreted accordingly. He also favored friendlier relations with France than with Great Britain because France had supported the United States in the Revolutionary War against Great Britain.

**Democrat Party, 1828-Present, (22 of 47 won (47%):** The third political party formed was the Democrat Party. It was led by Andrew Jackson who defected from the Democratic-Republican Party and ran against the Democratic-Republican candidate for president in 1828. Jackson thought that the Democratic-Republican Party had drifted away from the principles of Thomas Jefferson. The Democrat Party has been in existence ever since. It has had a major influence on the policies of the United States since its founding and today leans toward political liberalism.

**Whig Party, 1836-1852, (2 of 5 won (40%):** The fourth political party organized was the Whig Party. It was formed to contest Jackson's Democrat Party in the absence of the Democratic-Republican Party which had dissolved after losing to Jackson twice. The Whig Party favored a more powerful Congress than the presidency and was for a protective tariff to encourage the growth of American business. It also favored a strong central bank. The Whigs broke up over the question of slavery. It was replaced by the Republican Party in the presidential elections that followed.

**Republican Party, 1856-Present, 23 of 40 won (57%):** The Republican Party was founded after the collapse of the Whig Party. The Republican Party was first organized on the basis of being against slavery. Since its founding, all the presidential elections in the United States have been held between the Republican Party and the Democrat Party. In the first such election in 1856, Republican John C. Fremont was beaten by Democrat James Buchanan. Republican Abraham Lincoln won the next two elections. The Republican Party remains a major influence on the policies of the United States leaning toward political conservatism.

# The Presidents

**George Washington, 1st President, 1788-1796:** George Washington is called the "Father of our Country".

He was the first president as well as being the Commander of the Army that, against all odds, defeated the British gaining the colonies their independence. He was the president of the convention that wrote the American Constitution. He served two terms as President of the United States then retired from politics.

George's cabinet contained three of the most famous men in U.S. history: Vice-President John Adams, Secretary of State Thomas Jefferson, and Secretary of the Treasury Alexander Hamilton.

Washington sent John Jay to Great Britain to negotiate a treaty which averted war and started a prosperous trade between the two countries that lasted for years. (See the following three pages for more information on George Washington.)

Modern Day Contemporary: George Washington, the first president, was a born leader and a man of high moral character. He ran a plantation (farmed); loved his country; fought for his country; and led his country. The modern day president that most typifies George Washington is thought to be Dwight David Eisenhower, the 34<sup>th</sup> president. Although not a farmer originally, Eisenhower grew up in the farm country of Kansas and retired as a farmer. He graduated from West Point and probably had the most distinguished military career of anyone since Washington. Eisenhower loved his country and became a two term president like Washington. He retired after the presidency to his Gettysburg Farm in Pennsylvania.

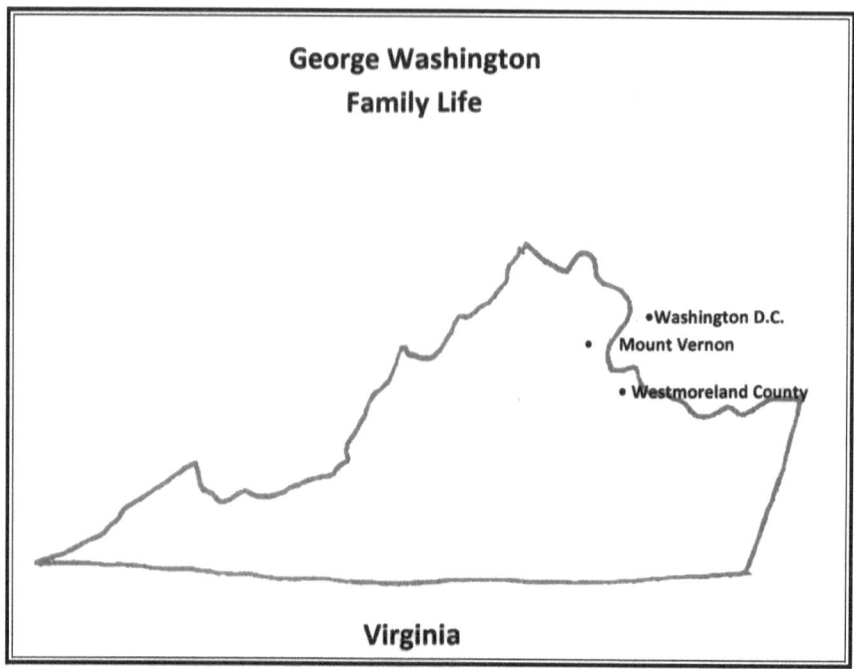

George Washington was born on February 22, 1732, in Westmoreland County, Virginia on the Potomac River not too far from Washington D.C. (The shape of the state of Virginia shown above is not the original but has existed since 1863 when West Virginia separated and joined the Union.) George was the eldest of six children born to Augustine and Mary Ball Washington. Prior to that, Augustine had four children by his first wife Jane Butler Washington who died in 1729. Later in life, George inherited and operated Mount Vernon plantation, a short distance up the Potomac River close to Washington D.C.. On January 6, 1759, George married Martha Dandridge Curtis, a widow. They had no children; however, George treated her two children, John and Martha, from a previous marriage as his own.

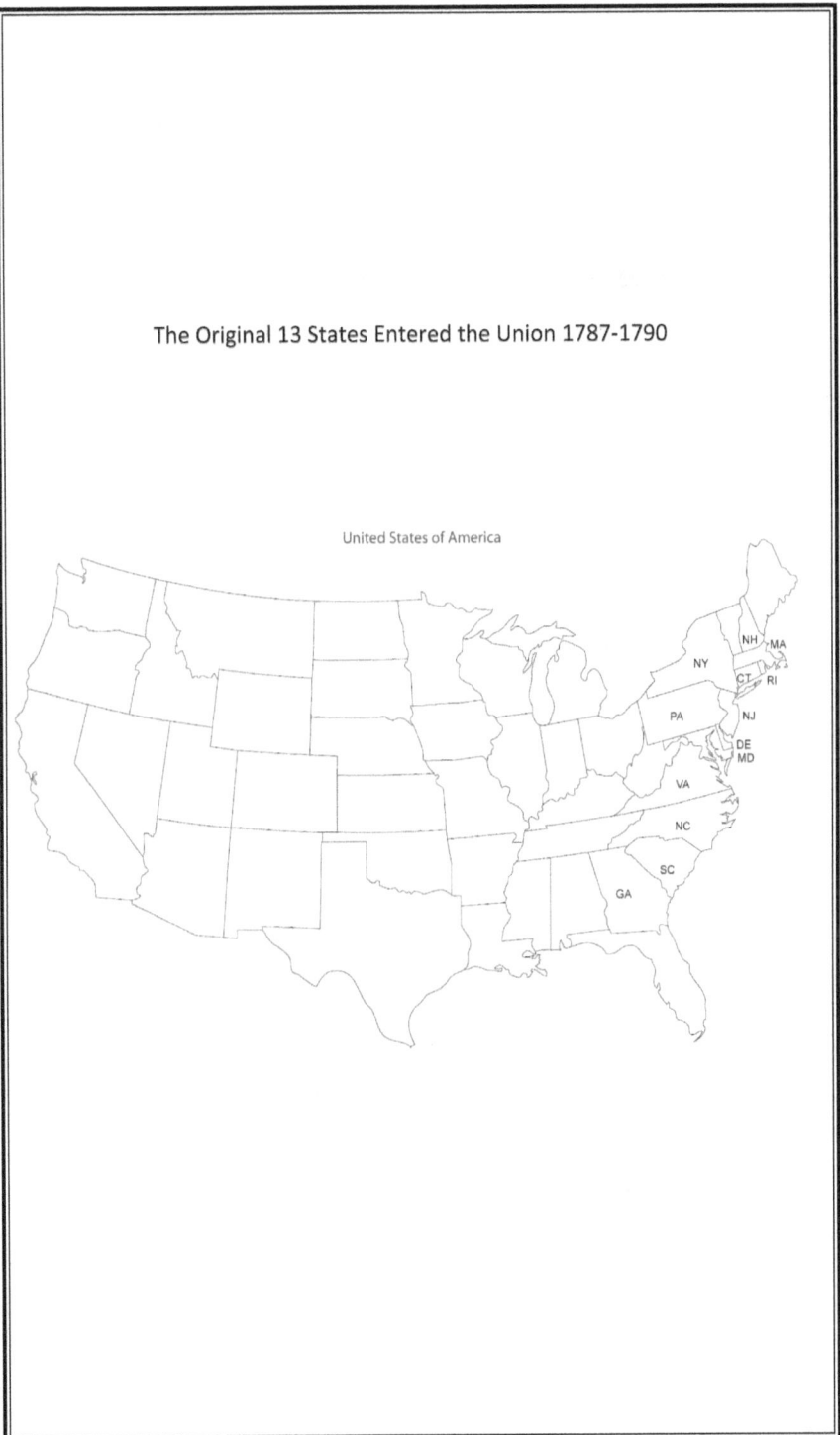

The Original 13 States Entered the Union 1787-1790

United States of America

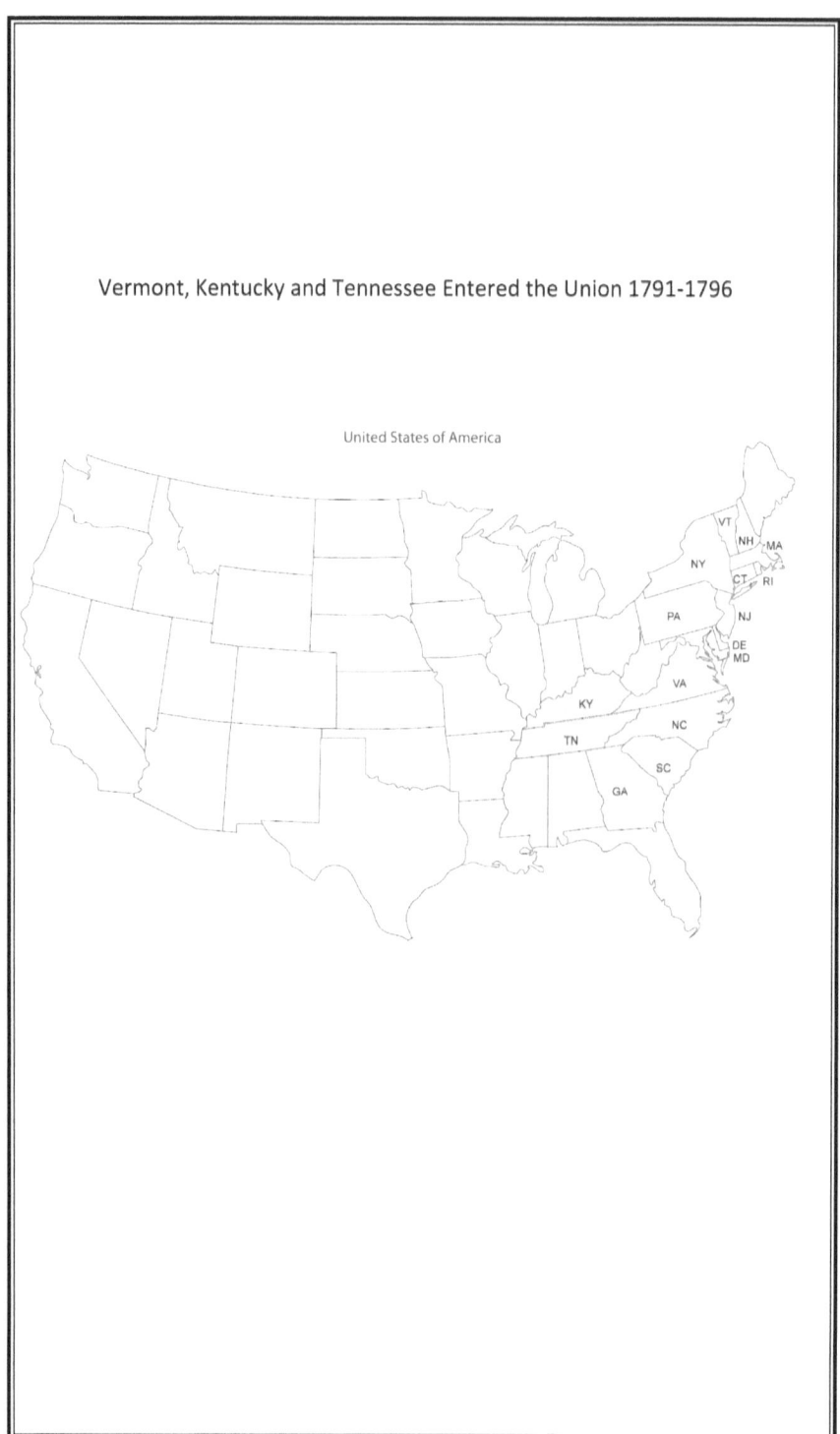

Vermont, Kentucky and Tennessee Entered the Union 1791-1796

United States of America

**John Adams, 2nd President, 1796-1800:** John Adams was born in Quincy, Massachusetts and graduated from Harvard. He established a law practice in Boston and defended the British soldiers who took part in the "Boston Massacre". His oldest son, John Quincy Adams, became the sixth president of the United States.

Adams became a leading opponent of Britain's attempts to tax the colonies. He was a member of the first Continental Congress and a fierce fighter for independence of the Colonies from England. He was appointed a member of the committee that drafted the Declaration of Independence and was George Washington's Vice-President for both terms.

In the presidential election of 1796, Adams defeated Jefferson by only three electoral votes. In the next election, Jefferson beat Adams by eight electoral votes.

Adams' term in office was characterized by a sharply divided country on whether to be a friend or foe of France. France was attacking American shipping because the United States had made peace with their enemy, Great Britain. At Adams urging, a peace treaty was signed with France ending all naval conflicts.

Modern Day Contemporary: It is difficult to select a modern day president or politician who has the love of country, tenacity, and temperament of John Adams. One might consider Harry Truman, 33rd President, who himself was the Vice-President of a great president (Roosevelt). Truman, like Adams, could be feisty at times. On more than one occasion, he wasn't afraid to chastise those individuals who criticized his daughter Margaret's musical talents. He is also credited with coining the phrase, "The buck stops here.", in describing himself as being the final authority on all political matters.

John Adams was born in Braintree (now Quincy) Massachusetts on October 30, 1735. His father was a farmer, militia officer, and church deacon. His mother was Susan Boylston Adams who came from a leading family of Boston physicians and merchants. In 1755, Adams graduated from Harvard. In 1764, he married Abigail Smith, the daughter of a minister. They moved to Boston where John became a prominent New England lawyer. They had four children. Their son, John Quincy Adams, became the sixth president of the United States one year before his father's passing.

**Thomas Jefferson, 3rd President, 1800-1808:** Next to George Washington, Thomas Jefferson is probably the most famous of all early Americans. Jefferson was born in Shadwell, Virginia, attended the College of William and Mary, and practiced law in Virginia. He was made a member of the committee, along with John Adams and Benjamin Franklin that drafted the "Declaration of Independence". Jefferson was elected Governor of Virginia and then appointed the first Secretary of State by George Washington. In 1796, Democratic-Republican Jefferson lost the presidency to Federalist John Adams by three electoral votes. In 1800, Jefferson beat Adams for the same post by eight electoral votes. In 1804, Jefferson Beat Federalist candidate Charles Pinckney for the presidency by an overwhelming majority of 162 to 14 votes.

A major achievement of Jefferson's first term in office was acquiring the "Louisiana Purchase" from France for 15 million dollars. This large tract of land stretched from the Mississippi River to the Rocky Mountains and doubled the size of the U.S.. During Jefferson's second term, war again broke out between Britain and France with both countries attacking American shipping. He sponsored "The Embargo Act" which closed all American ports to shipping both domestic and foreign.

After he retired, Jefferson renewed his acquaintance with his old friend and political rival, John Adams. Both men died on the same day, July 4, 1826, the 50th anniversary of the day they both signed the Declaration of Independence.

<u>Modern Day Contemporary</u>: The modern day person that most reminds one of Jefferson is thought to be Lyndon Johnson, 36th president. Both were southerners and were tough at the bargaining table where they dedicated themselves to the plight of the individual citizen and both were in office when military conflicts plagued the country.

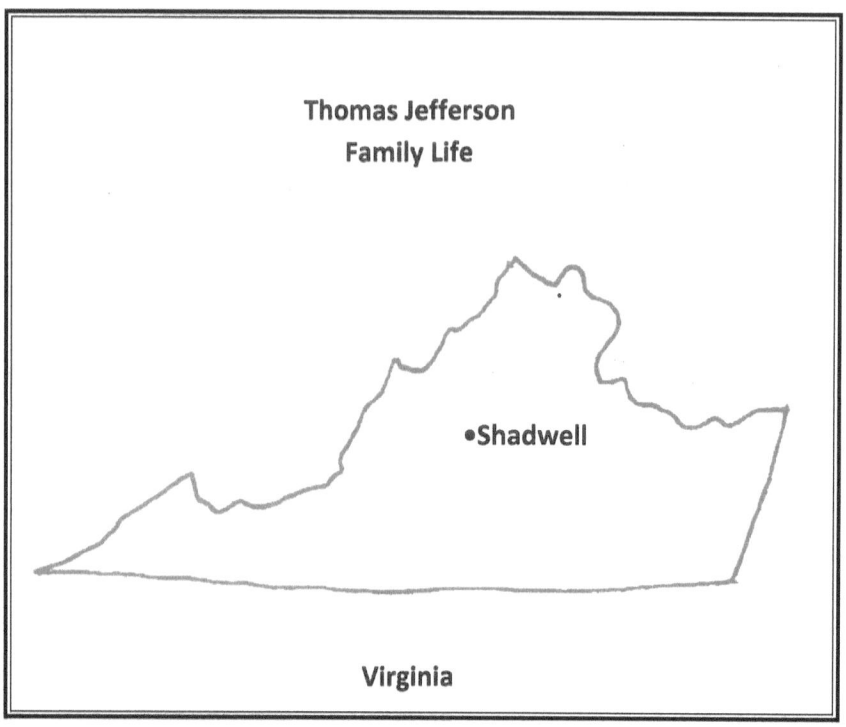

**Thomas Jefferson Family Life**

•Shadwell

**Virginia**

Thomas Jefferson was born in Shadwell, Albemarle County, Virginia (near Charlottesville) on April 13, 1743. He was the third child in a family of ten. His father was a member of the House of Burgesses while his mother, Jane Randolph Jefferson, was from a long line of Virginians. Jefferson's father died when he was 14 years old leaving him, the eldest son, ownership of the 2500 acre estate. He graduated from college and went on to practice law. In 1772, Thomas married Martha Wayles Skelton, the daughter of a prominent lawyer. They lived at Monticello, Jefferson's new home on his estate in Shadwell. They had six children with only two, Martha and Mary, living to adulthood. Mrs. Jefferson died in 1782 after being married only ten years. Her death haunted Thomas and he never remarried.

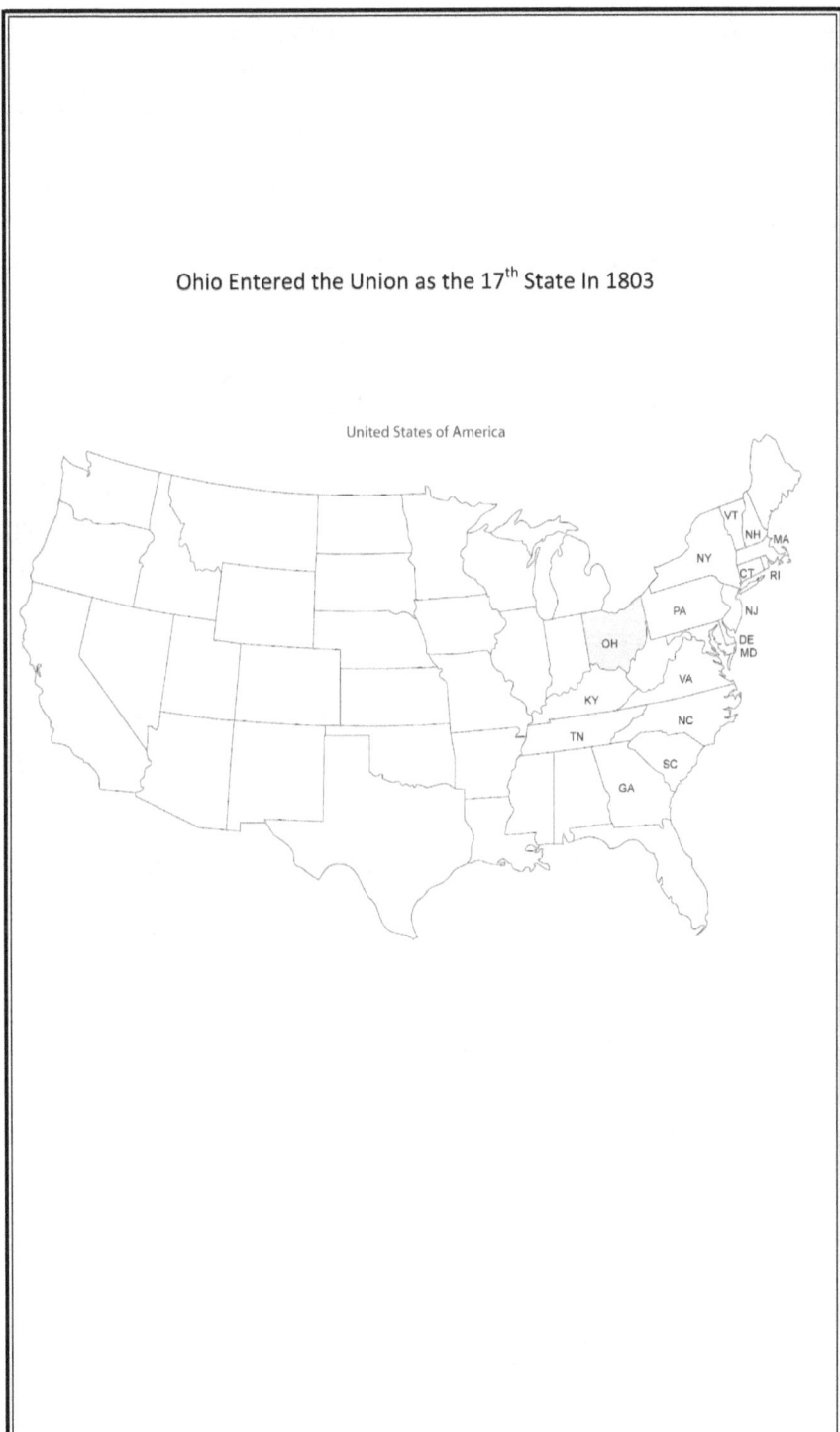

Ohio Entered the Union as the 17<sup>th</sup> State In 1803

United States of America

**James Madison, 4th President, 1808-1816:** James Madison was born near Port Conway, Virginia. Growing up he was rather frail and sickly; however, he studied diligently under various tutors in Virginia and also at Princeton University. He grew to five feet four inches tall weighing only 100 pounds. When Madison was 43 years old, he married 26 year old Dolly Payne Todd, a widow. Dolly knew her way around Washington and was to become a famous first lady entertaining guests at the White House.

James Madison was a member of the Continental Congress. In 1787, a national convention was called; and, using Madison's plan, the Constitution of the United States was written. Madison has since been called "The Father of the Constitution". Madison became a member of the U.S. House of Representatives where he took a leading role in getting the first ten amendments passed. He was Secretary of State from 1800 to 1808 under President Thomas Jefferson. Jefferson then chose Madison to succeed him as president. Madison beat Federalist candidate Charles Pinckney, a South Carolina lawyer and former Minister to France for the high office. Thomas Jefferson had beaten Pinckney in the previous election. Madison beat Federalist candidate DeWitt Clinton, Mayor of New York, for his second term.

The War of 1812 took place against Great Britain during Madison's reign. For years, the British were raiding American vessels on the high seas. Madison tried to steer a neutral course but was forced into war.

Modern Day Contemporary: One might suggest that a modern day contemporary of Madison be Jimmy Carter, 39th President. Both are relatively small in stature, well-educated southerners who championed individual rights. Also, both were involved in conflicts with foreign countries, Madison with Great Britain, Carter with Iran.

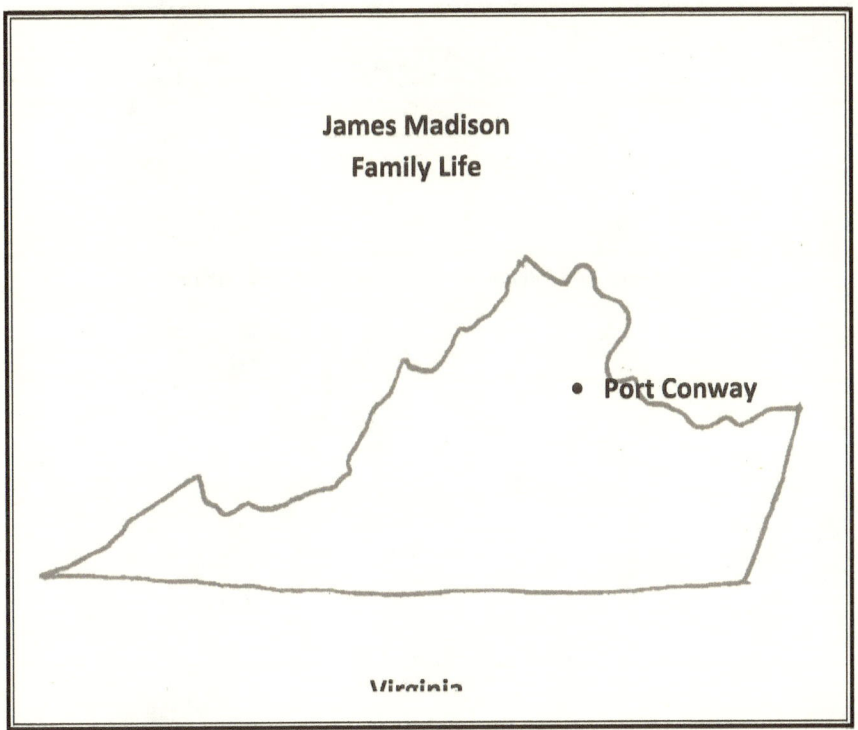

James Madison was born in Port Conway (near Fredericksburg), Virginia on March 16, 1751. He was the eldest of 12 children born to his parents, James Madison Sr. and Nelly Conway Madison. Both parents had deep roots in Virginia. He lived at the family plantation called Montpelier. He attended Princeton University and graduated in two years. In 1776, he was a member of Virginia's first state government where he met Thomas Jefferson. The two became lifelong friends.

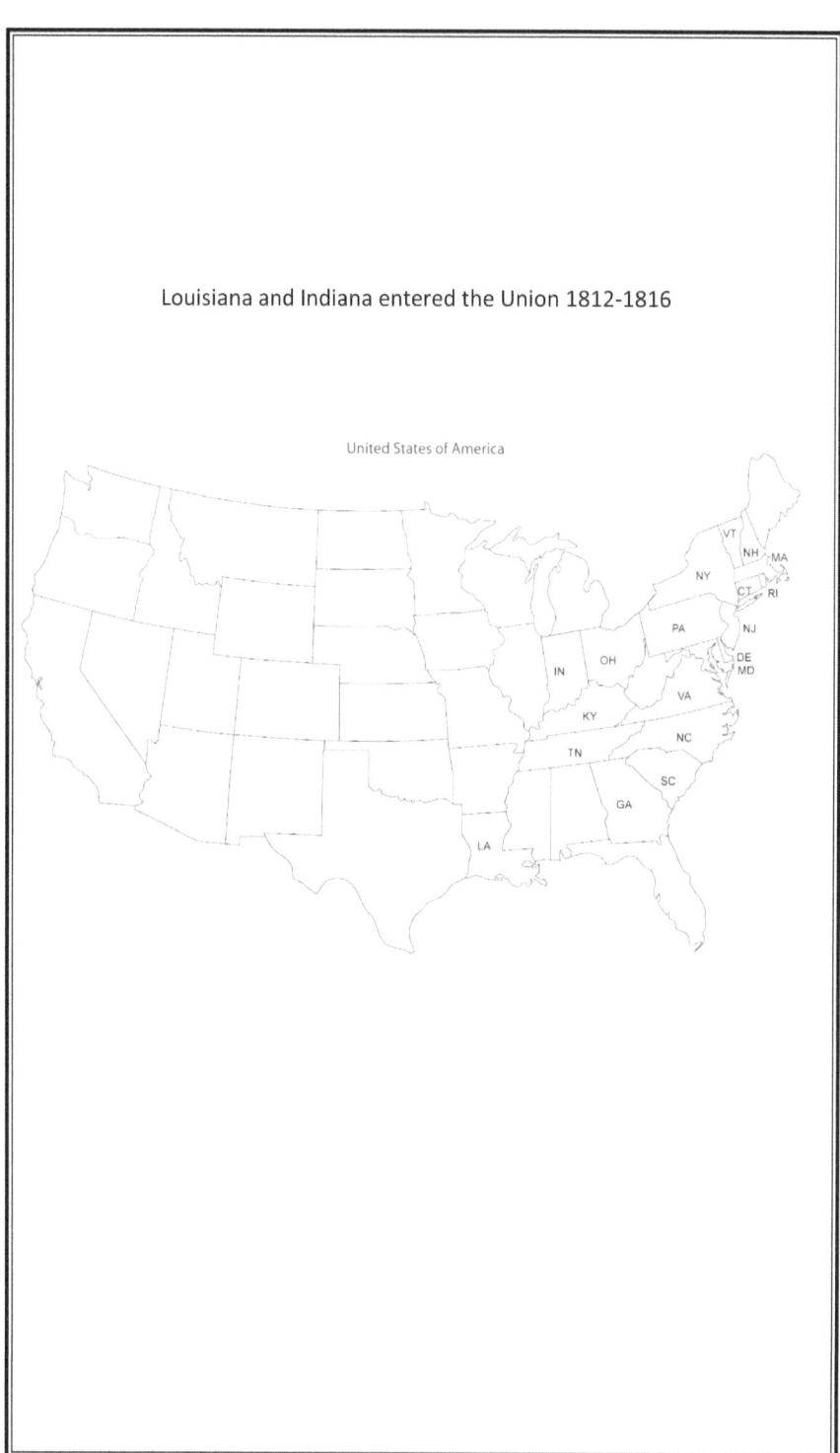

Louisiana and Indiana entered the Union 1812-1816

United States of America

**James Monroe, 5th President, 1816-1824:** James Monroe was born in Westmoreland County, Virginia; the third straight president born in Virginia.

At age 16, Monroe attended the college of William and Mary but left early to fight under George Washington in the Revolutionary War. After the war, he served in a number of important government positions both in the U.S. and abroad before becoming Secretary of State under Madison.

In the election of 1816, Democratic-Republican Monroe beat Federalist Rufus B. King. The three Virginians: Jefferson, Madison, and Monroe, so dominated politics in their era that the Federalist Party they ran against ceased to exist and Monroe ran unopposed his second term.

Achievements made during Monroe's presidency were the 1820 Missouri Compromise and the 1823 Monroe Doctrine. After Monroe ordered General Andrew Jackson to end an uprising in Georgia and Florida, the U.S. purchased Florida for five million dollars from Spain. With Great Britain, he established the common boundary that exists today between the U.S. and Canada. He convinced Spain and Russia to give up claims to Oregon. James Monroe is probably one of the most underrated of all U.S. presidents.

Modern Day Contemporary: Unfortunately, there is thought to be no modern day government official who has had James Monroe's achievements; although, in fairness to all, opportunities in the United States do not exist today that James Monroe had success dealing with during his time as president.

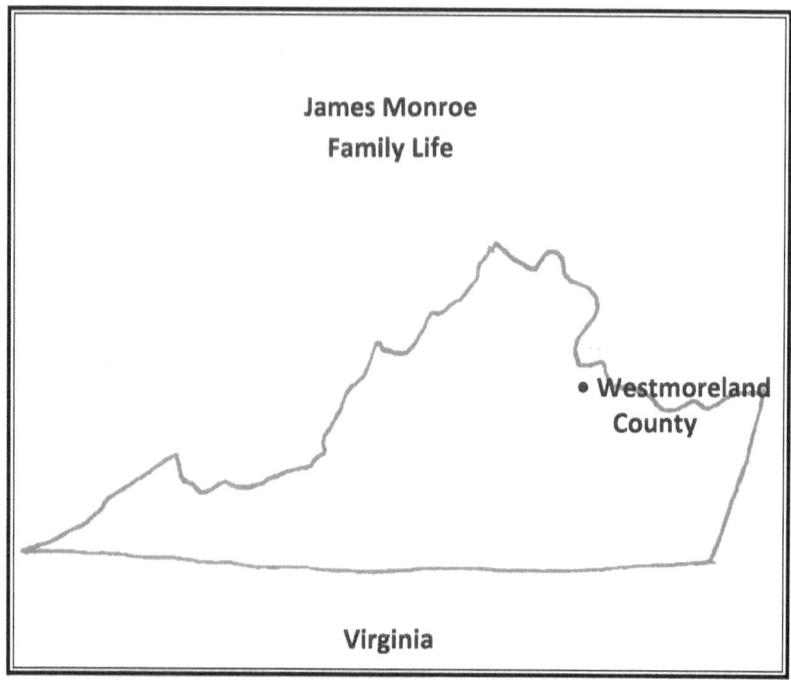

James Monroe was born in Westmoreland County, Virginia on April 28, 1758. His father, Colonel Spence Monroe, and his mother, Elizabeth Jones Monroe, both came from families that were early settlers of Virginia. When he was just 16 years, he entered the College of William and Mary; however, the Revolutionary War lured him into the army before he could graduate. He was wounded and cited for gallantry in action. He studied law under Thomas Jefferson and the two became lifelong friends.

Mississippi, Illinois, Alabama, Maine and Missouri

Entered the Union 1817-1821

**John Quincy Adams, 6th President, 1824-1828:** John Quincy Adams was the eldest son of the second president of the United States, John Adams. He graduated from Harvard and practiced law in Boston.

Adams held several important government positions at home and abroad and later, after changing from being a Federalist to a Democratic-Republican, became Monroe's Secretary of State

There were four candidates for the presidency in 1824, and all four were Democratic-Republicans. Andrew Jackson received 99 electoral votes, Adams 84, William Crawford 41, and Henry Clay 37. Since no one held a majority, the House of Representatives had to choose among the top three contenders putting Henry Clay out of the race. Clay supported Adams who won making Clay Secretary of State. This greatly angered Andrew Jackson who said it was a "crooked deal".

During his presidency, Adams proposed a national university, a national observatory, and a vast federal roads program; but, Congress, supported by opposition from Andrew Jackson, defeated them.

Modern Day Contemporary: One might think that George W. Bush, 43rd president, and the only son of a president to be elected to the presidency after Adams, might be considered somewhat of a contemporary to Adams. Like Adams, Bush had fierce opposition from the opposing party while in office. Unlike Adams, Bush was able to be elected to a second term.

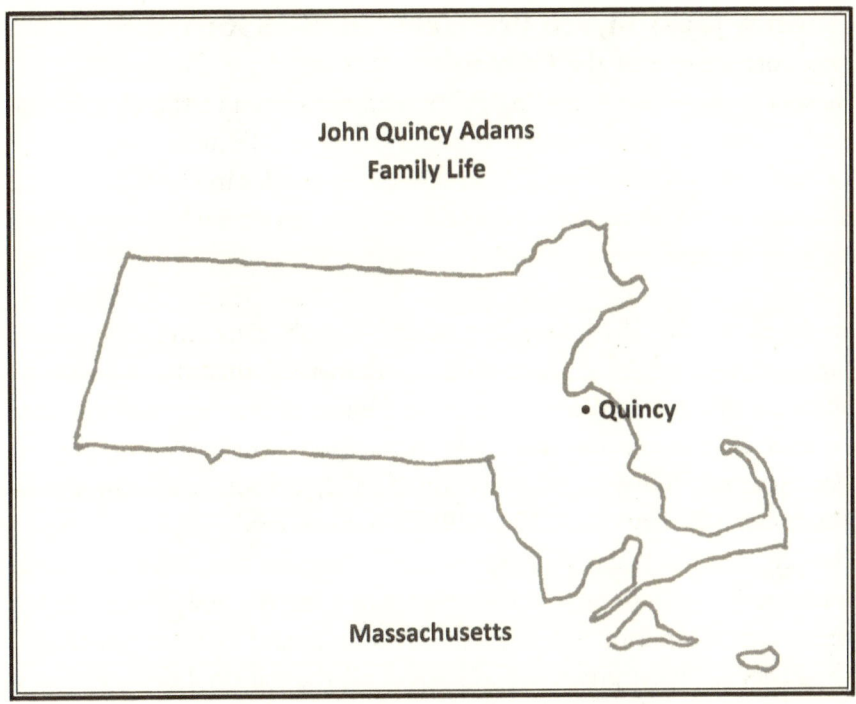

John Quincy Adams
Family Life

• Quincy

Massachusetts

John Quincy Adams was born in Quincy, Massachusetts on July 11, 1767. He was the eldest son of his father, John Adams who was the second president of the United States. He spent his early life traveling to various European countries with his father, who was a diplomat. He attended various schools in Europe then came home and entered Harvard where he graduated in two years. He practiced law and became a political journalist. Just after becoming Minister to Prussia for his father, Johnson married Louisa Catherine Johnson in 1797. They had four children. His youngest son, Charles Francis, served as Minister to Great Britain during the Civil War.

**Andrew Jackson, 7th President, 1828-1836:** Andrew Jackson was born in one of the Carolinas. Both states have claimed him but he said it was South Carolina (Waxhall). He served in the U.S. House and Senate and was elected Major General of the Tennessee militia. He offered his services to the U.S. and won key battles in the War of 1812 against the British in Alabama and New Orleans after which he became a national hero.

In the election of 1824, four Democratic-Republicans ran for president. Jackson received more electoral votes than the other three; however, since no one received a majority, the House of Representatives chose Adams. In the next election in 1828, Jackson, after changing parties, beat Adams 178 to 83. In the election of 1832, Jackson beat Democratic-Republican Henry Clay 219 to 49. Historians' credit Jackson as being the originator of today's Democrat Party. Jackson said in his inaugural address: "The Federal Constitution must be obeyed; states' rights preserved; our national debt paid; direct taxes and loans avoided; and, the Federal Union preserved". He paid off the national debt; the only president ever to do so. When France failed to make its first payment for damages made to American shipping during the Napoleonic Wars, he asked Congress for increased military expenditures. After that, France made four back payments with interest. President Andrew Jackson was a man who backed up his words with action.

Modern Day Contemporary: A modern day person thought to be a contemporary of Andrew Jackson is General George S. Patton. Both were of southern heritage and highly opinionated. Both were born military leaders and both won brilliant victories on the battlefield; however, Patton never had a chance to become president as he died in an automobile accident in Europe just after World War II.

Andrew Jackson
Family Life

• Waxhaw

South Carolina

There is a debate on where Andrew Jackson was born whether it is in North Carolina or South Carolina. He has said that he was born on his Uncle James Crawford's farm near Waxhaw, South Carolina, just inside the state border with North Carolina. He was born on March 15, 1767. His parents, Andrew and Elizabeth Hutchinson Jackson, were poor farmers who came from Northern Ireland with their first two sons. Andrew Jackson senior died in 1767 just a few days before Andrew junior was born. The family moved in with Mrs. Jackson's sister, Mrs. Jane Crawford. Jackson joined the South Carolina militia during the Revolutionary War when he was just 13 years old. Later in life he became a lawyer and was appointed Attorney General of the territory that is now Tennessee. Jackson married Mrs. Rachel Donelson Robards, a divorcee, in August, 1791. They remarried on January 17, 1794 when it was learned that Mrs. Robards may not have been divorced as they had previously thought. They had no children of their own but raised three of Mrs. Jackson's relative's children.

# Arkansas Entered the Union as the 25<sup>th</sup> State in 1836

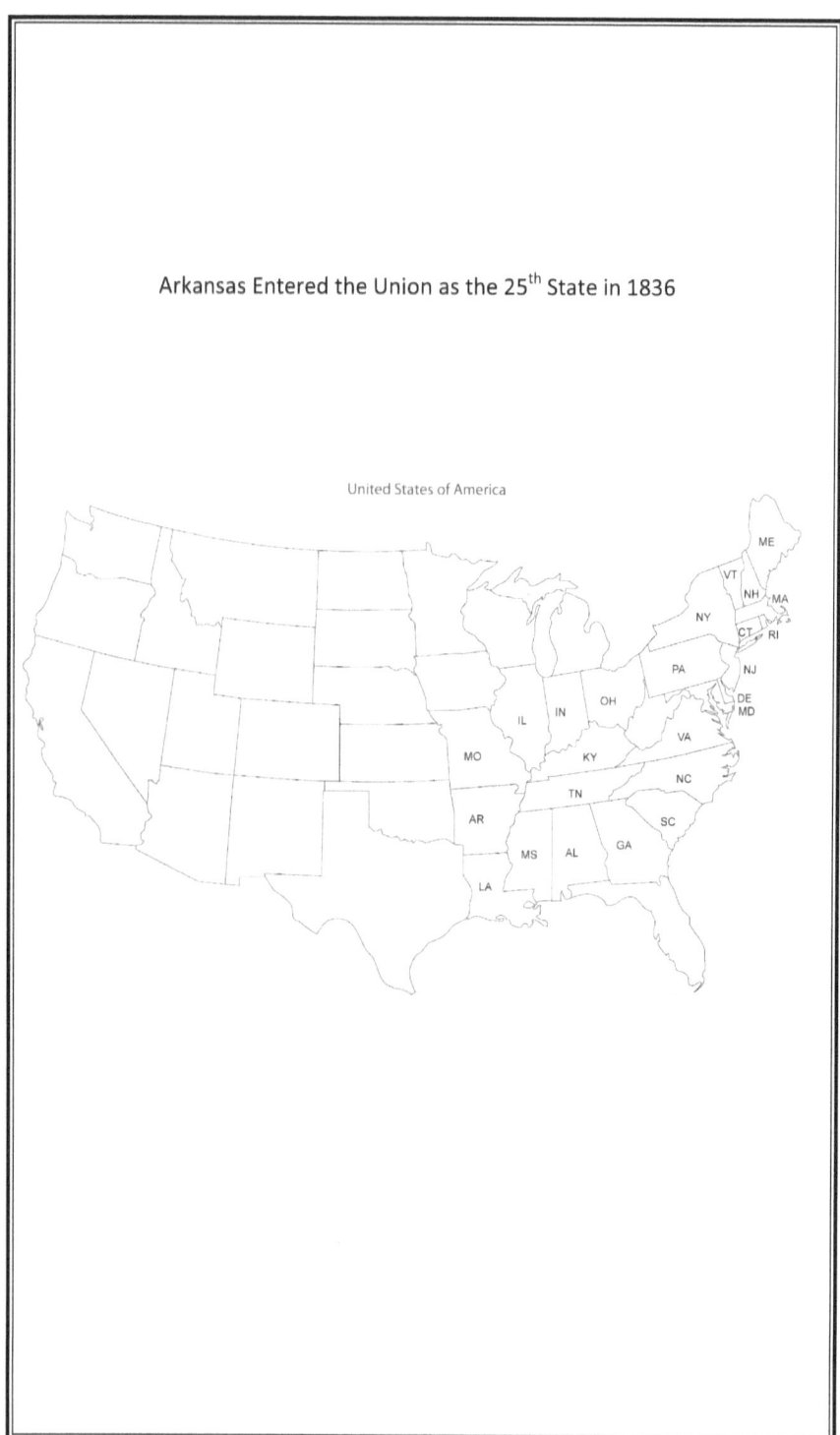

United States of America

**Martin Van Buren, 8th President, 1836-1840:** Martin Van Buren was born in Kinderhook, New York.

He served in the U.S. Senate and later as Secretary of State and Vice President under Andrew Jackson.

In the election of 1836, Democrat Martin Van Buren beat Whig candidate William Henry Harrison by an electoral vote count of 170 to 73. In the following election, Van Buren lost to the same man by an electoral vote count of 234 to 60. The Democrats picked James K. Polk as their candidate for the election in 1844.

Unfortunately, Van Buren presided over the country during its first great depression which hit in 1837.

In 1840, William Henry Harrison said that Van Buren showed a lack of compassion toward the people. The same man that Van Buren beat badly in the previous election now won by an electoral vote count of 234 to 60.

Modern Day Contemporary: A modern day contemporary to Van Buren may be Herbert Hoover, 31st President of the United States, even though they were in competing political parties. When in office, each one was besieged by the country being hit by a great depression and each was criticized for not doing enough in providing aid to the many people who were affected by the economic downturn.

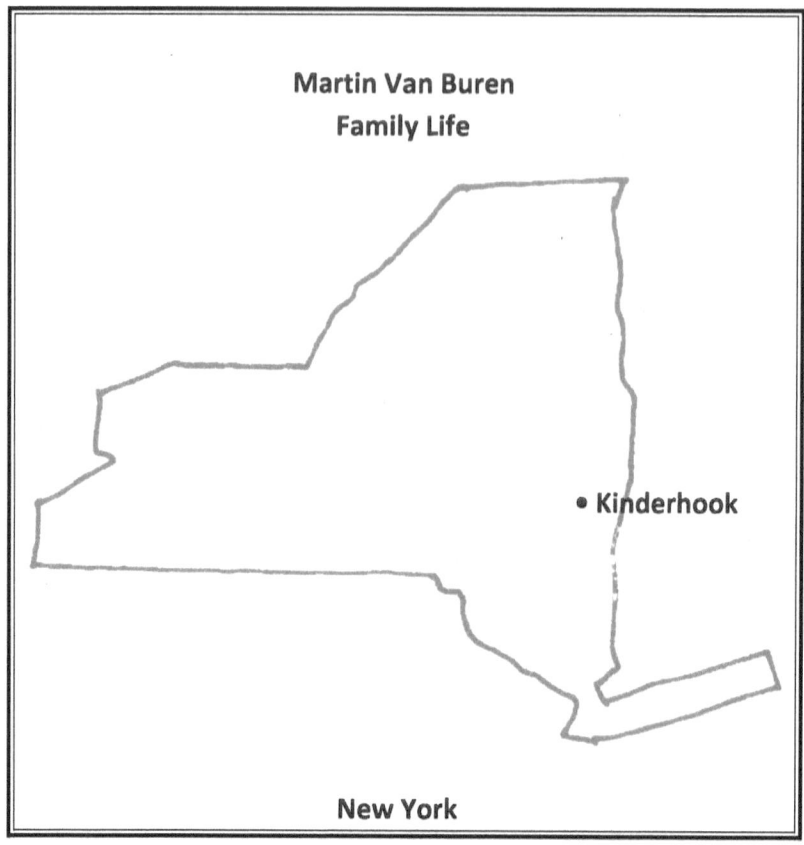

**Martin Van Buren**
**Family Life**

• Kinderhook

**New York**

Martin Van Buren was born in Kinderhook, New York, on December 5, 1782. He was the third of five children born to Dutch parents Abraham and Maria Hoes Van Buren. Martin's father ran a truck farm and a tavern. Martin studied law and first took part in a court case when he was 15 years old. He married his distant cousin, Hannah Hoes on February 21, 1807. They had four sons: Abraham, the oldest became his father's secretary at the White House while John, the second son, became Attorney General of New York.

# Michigan Entered the Union as the 26<sup>th</sup> State in 1837

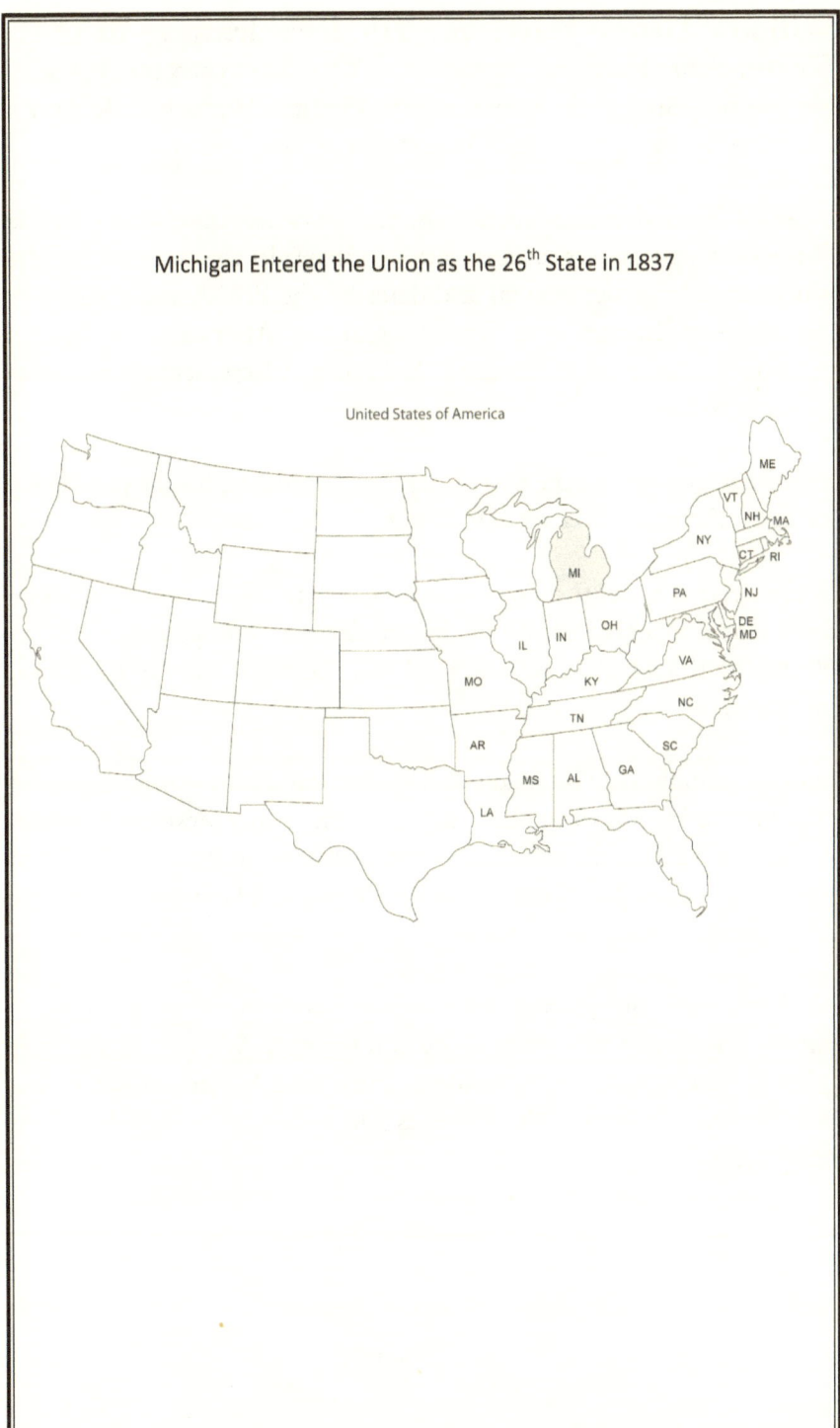

United States of America

## William Henry Harrison, 9th President, 1840-1841:

William Henry Harrison was the fourth Virginian to become president. He was born in Charles City County, Virginia. His father, Benjamin Harrison, was a signer of the Declaration of Independence.

In 1811, Tyler defeated Tecumseh, the Shawnee tribe leader in the Battle of Tippecanoe near Lafayette, Indiana. In the war of 1812, he was made a brigadier general and defeated the British and Indians in the Battle of Thames near Ontario, Canada. Afterwards, he settled in Ohio where he served in the U.S. House of Representatives and as Minister to Columbia.

In 1836, Harrison was the first Whig Party candidate for the presidency losing to Democrat Martin Van Buren.

In the election of 1840, using the famous slogan "Tippecanoe and Tyler too", Harrison beat Van Buren by an electoral vote count of 234 to 60. At the time, he was 68 years old and the oldest man to be elected president.

Harrison caught cold on inauguration day and died one month later of pneumonia. He was to serve the shortest term of any president in office, 31 days, preventing the initiation of any legislative action. Vice President John Tyler succeeded him. Grandson Benjamin Harrison became the 23 president of the United States.

Modern Day Contemporary: Although they were in competing political parties, the closest one that can be compared to William Harrison is John F. Kennedy, the 35th President. Both were Easterners' who went on to become famous military heroes and both died in their first term of office.

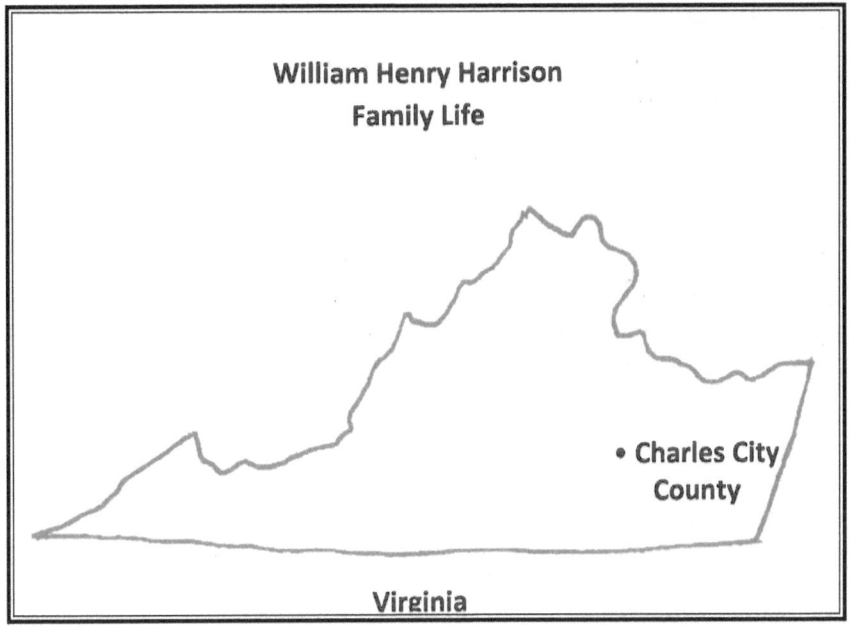

William Henry Harrison was born in Charles City County, Virginia on February 9, 1773 at his father's Berkeley plantation. His parents were Benjamin and Elizabeth Basset Harrison. Benjamin had served in the Continental Congress and was a signer of the Declaration of Independence. Harrison quit studying medicine and joined the army. He became commander of Fort Washington, Ohio where he met his wife, Anna Symmes. They had ten children with six of them dying before Harrison became president. He was appointed secretary of the Northwest Territory by President John Adams. He won a famous battle at the Tippecanoe River in Indiana against the Shawnee chief Tecumseh to open up treaty acquired land for settlement.

**John Tyler, 10th President, 1841-1844:** John Tyler, the tenth president, was the fifth Virginian to ascend to the high office. He was born in Charles City County, Virginia.

He became governor of Virginia and U.S. Representative and Senator before being elected vice-president in 1840

Tyler became the 10th president when William Henry Harrison, the 9th president, became ill and died 31 days after his inauguration. After serving the remainder of the term, Tyler did not run for the presidency in 1844.

While in office, Tyler found himself being against some of the Whig Party platform. As a result, most of his cabinet resigned and he was expelled from the Whig Party; nevertheless, he established the United States Weather Department; reorganized the navy; and put an end to the Second Seminole War in Florida.

Tyler was elected to the Confederate House of Representatives but died in 1862 before he could be seated.

Modern Day Contemporary: It is hard to find a modern day contemporary to John Tyler because of the unusual series of events that surrounded him. He quit the Democrat Party to join the Whig Party and when elected, did not agree with the Whig platform. This has not been the case with any of today's presidents.

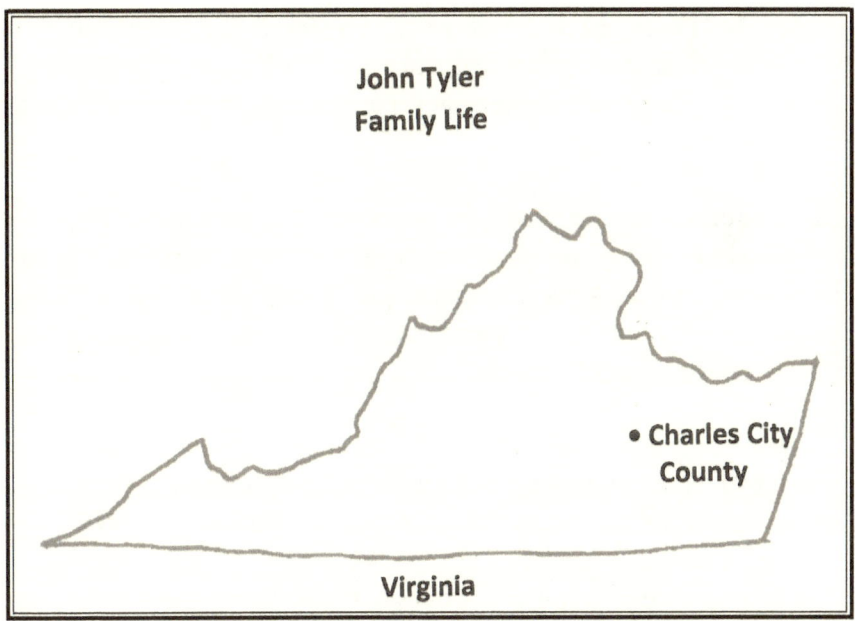

John Tyler and President William Henry Harrison he served under were both born in Charles City County, Virginia. Tyler was born on March 29, 1790, the son of John and Mary Armistead Tyler. His father was Speaker of the Virginia House of Delegates and Governor of Virginia. John junior graduated from the College of William and Mary at the age of 17. He became a lawyer; a member of the Virginia House of Delegates; and a captain in the War of 1812. He married Letitia Christian on March 29, 1813 and they had eight children. Letitia died during her husband's presidency. He remarried 22 months later.

**James K. Polk, 11th President, 1844-1848:** James Polk was born in Pineville, North Carolina and moved to Tennessee when he was 10 years old. There he became a lawyer and supported Andrew Jackson for the presidency

The Democrat Party surprised the nation with its nomination of James K. Polk as the presidential candidate for the 1844 election. Initially, the delegation could not agree between ex-president Martin Van Buren and former Minister to France, Lewis Cass. Polk's name was suggested and he won on the next (8th) ballot.

The Whigs nominated Henry Clay for president. Clay had already been beaten by Democrat Andrew Jackson in 1832. Polk won the election by about 40,000 popular votes. He did not seek reelection in 1848.

Polk was accused of not looking out for the interests of the poor; but, his achievements were noteworthy. He set four goals to meet during his term and he was to accomplish all four. He had a law passed which reduced tariffs. He created an independent Treasury which handled federal funds. It was to last until 1913 when the Federal Reserve System was created. He signed a treaty with Great Britain establishing the 49th parallel as the Oregon Territory boundary with Canada. He went to war with Mexico and claimed the land which is now Arizona, California, Colorado, Nevada, New Mexico, Utah, and Wyoming

Modern Day Contemporary: No modern day president has had the opportunities and achievements that Polk had preventing any comparison that can be made.

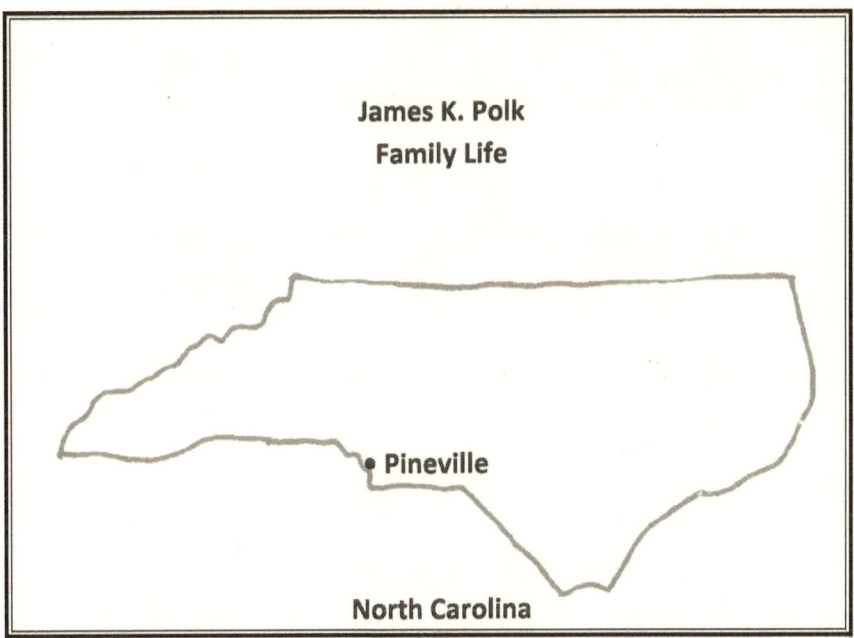

**James K. Polk**
**Family Life**

• Pineville

**North Carolina**

James K. Polk was born near Pineville, North Carolina on November 2, 1795. His family moved to Tennessee when he was ten years old. He was the son of Samuel and Jane Knox Polk. The Polks emigrated from Ireland. James was the eldest of ten children. He graduated from the University of North Carolina at the top of his class. Polk married Sarah Childress on January 1, 1824. They had no children. Andrew Jackson (Old Hickory) became such a friend that Polk was sometimes called "Young Hickory".

Florida, Texas, Iowa and Wisconsin Entered the Union 1845-1848

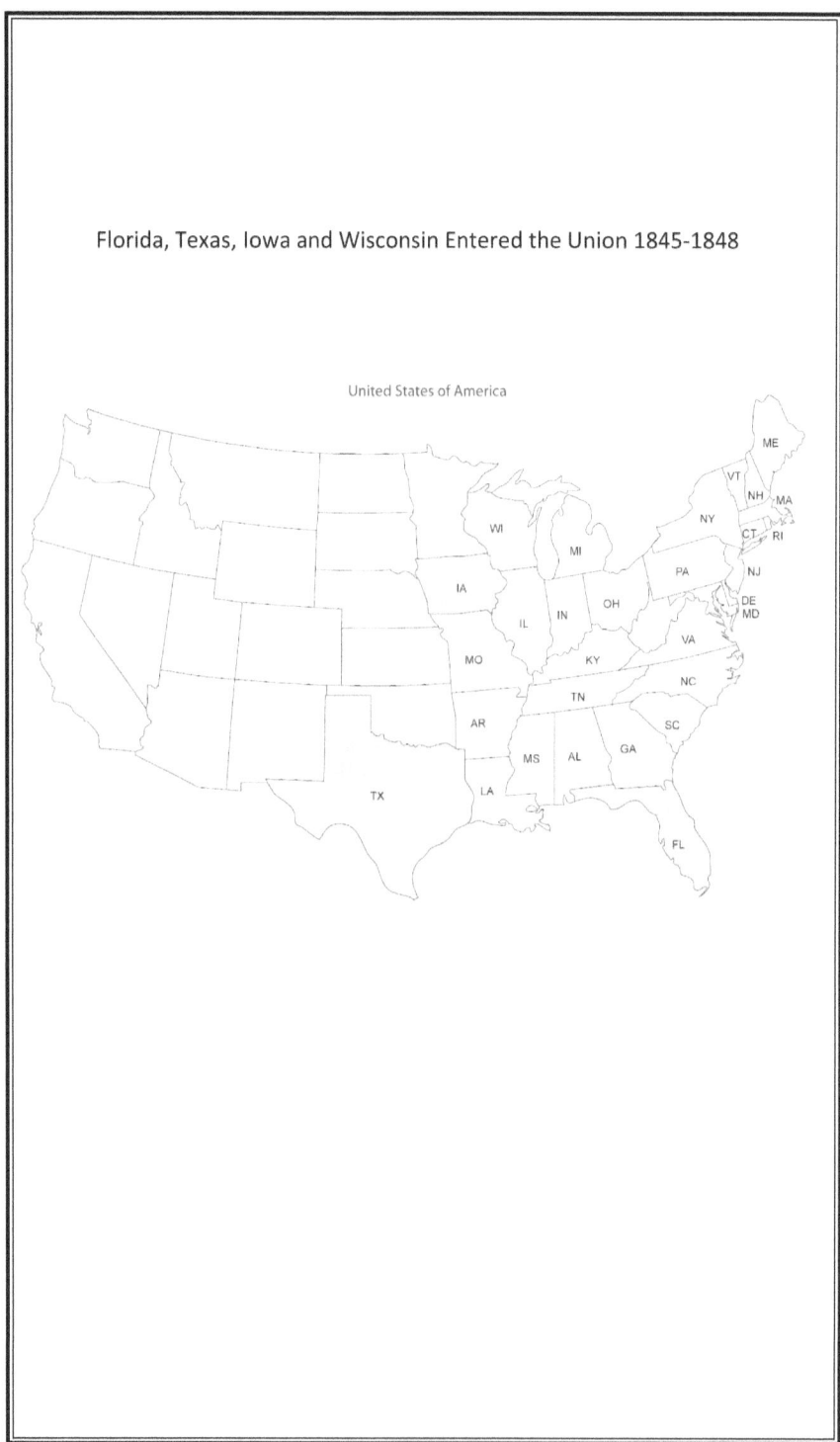

United States of America

**Zachary Taylor, 12th President, 1848-1850:** Zachary Taylor, the twelfth president, was born in Barboursville, Virginia; the sixth president born in Virginia; however, his family moved to Kentucky when he was an infant. He became a military man and was made general. He won a stunning victory in the Battle of Buena Vista, Mexico, in which his 5000 man army had been outnumbered by over a 3 to 1 margin by Santa Ana's forces.

In 1848, the Whig nominating convention selected Taylor as their candidate for the presidency. In the presidential election he narrowly defeated Democrat Lewis Cass. His victory was assisted by former Democratic President Martin Van Buren who ran as a Free Soil Party candidate taking away crucial votes from Cass.

Discussions over the slavery issue had been going on for four years and heated debates continued during Taylor's term. On July 4th, 1850, after attending Independence Day ceremonies at the Washington Monument, Taylor returned to the White House and had a snack. He became ill and died on July 9th of gastroenteritis (inflammation of the stomach and intestines.) The famous "Compromise of 1850" was passed temporarily settling the slavery issue for years. It was signed by newly appointed president, Willard Fillmore.

Modern Day Contemporary: One is reminded that a modern day contemporary to Zachary Taylor might be General Douglas MacArthur; both had southern blood; MacArthur's mother was from Virginia and his father from New Mexico. Taylor's nickname "Old Rough and Ready" could also be applied to MacArthur. MacArthur spent much of his life winning World War II battles for his country in the South Pacific. MacArthur would have been a good candidate for President except for having a major dispute with President Truman over post-World War II military strategy.

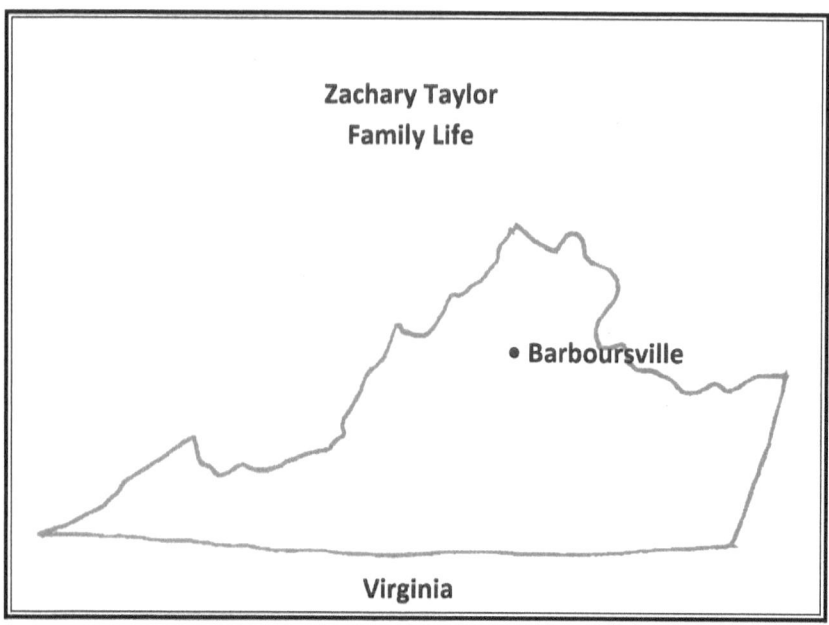

Zachary Taylor was born near Barboursville, Virginia on November 24, 1784, but grew up near Louisville, Kentucky. He was the son of Richard and Sarah Strother Taylor who came from the Virginia plantation region. Zachary was the third son in a family of nine. He married Margaret Mackall Smith on June 21, 1810. They had six children. Daughter Sarah married Jefferson Davis, who was to become President of the Confederacy. His son became a general in the Confederate army. Taylor had a distinguished military career culminating in a brilliant victory in the Mexican War over General Santa Anna's forces bringing him national fame.

California Entered the Union as the 31st State in 1850

United States of America

**Millard Fillmore, 13th President, 1850-1852:** Millard Fillmore was born in Moravia, New York and was a cloth maker before becoming a lawyer and being elected to the U.S. House of Representatives.

In the convention of 1848, the Whig Party nominated Taylor and Fillmore who beat Democrats Lewis Cass of Michigan and William Butler of Kentucky. Vice-President Millard Fillmore succeeded President Zachary Taylor who died after serving just 16 months in office. Fillmore was the second vice-president to be elevated to the top office

Fillmore took over the presidency when a fierce debate was still taking place over slavery in this country. California applied for admission into the Union as a free state. Southern pro-slavery forces threatened to secede and Northerners threatened war.

Congress passed a series of bills called the Compromise of 1850 which Fillmore gladly signed. It has been said that this great piece of legislation delayed the start of the Civil War by ten years.

In 1852, the Whigs nominated anti-slavery candidate General Winfield Scott over Fillmore as their presidential candidate.

Modern Day Contemporary: There is no modern day contemporary that has had to deal with a split country like what was handed to President Fillmore.

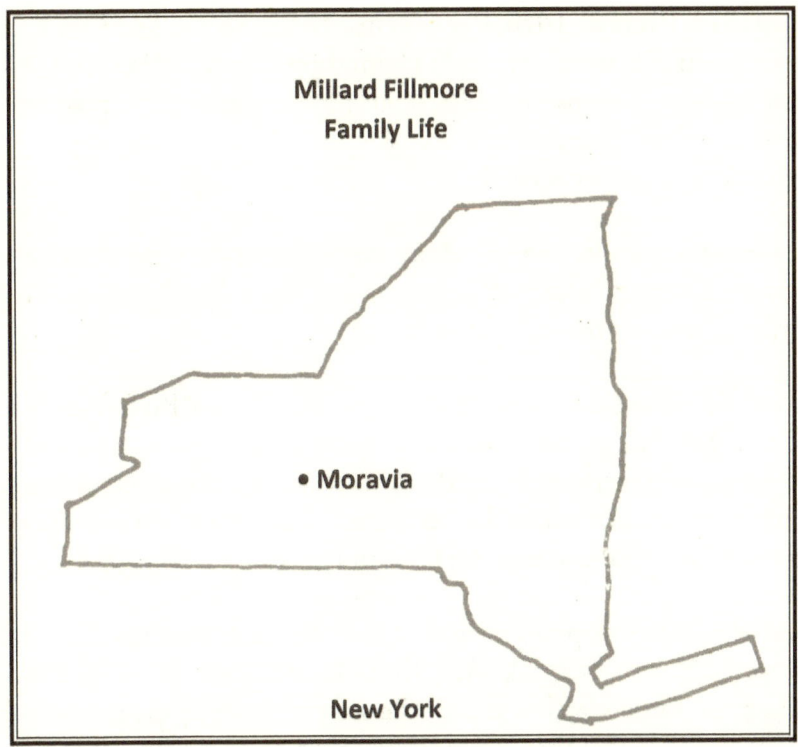

**Millard Fillmore
Family Life**

• **Moravia**

**New York**

Millard Fillmore was born on January 7, 1800, in Moravia, New York to Nathaniel and Phoebe Millard Fillmore. He was the second child in a family of nine. At an early age, Millard was a cloth maker then became a lawyer. He married Abigail Powers in 1826. They had two children and moved to Buffalo, New York. There he started his political career by being elected to the New York House of Representatives.

**Franklin Pierce, 14th President, 1852-1856:** Franklin Pierce was born in Hillsborough, New Hampshire; the only President to be born in New Hampshire. After college, he began a law practice in Concord, New Hampshire. Pierce enlisted in the service and rose to the rank of brigadier general.

In the primary election of 1852, the Democrats were deadlocked between Douglas, Marcy, Buchanan, and Cass. Pierce, regarded as a war hero, won on the 49th ballot.

In the national election of 1852, Pierce beat Whig Party candidate, General Winfield Scott of Virginia; the man he served under during the Mexican-American War. This was to be the last election for the Whig Party. Since then, all United States elections have been contested between the Democrat and Republican Parties.

President Pierce supported and signed Senator Stephen Douglas's sponsored Kansas-Nebraska Act. The bill established the two territories and let the settlers within decide the slavery issue. It was to upset the delicate balance that the Compromise of 1850 had provided on slavery. This issue ruined Pierce's career and he was not re-nominated in 1856.

The Gadsden Purchase was made during Pierce's term. The U.S. purchased a small strip of land from Mexico for ten million dollars. It forms the southern boundary of Arizona and New Mexico and provided the U.S. with an avenue to build a southern railroad to the Pacific Ocean.

Modern Day Contemporary: There can be found no modern day contemporary of Pierce because of the fierce debate over the slavery issue during his term.

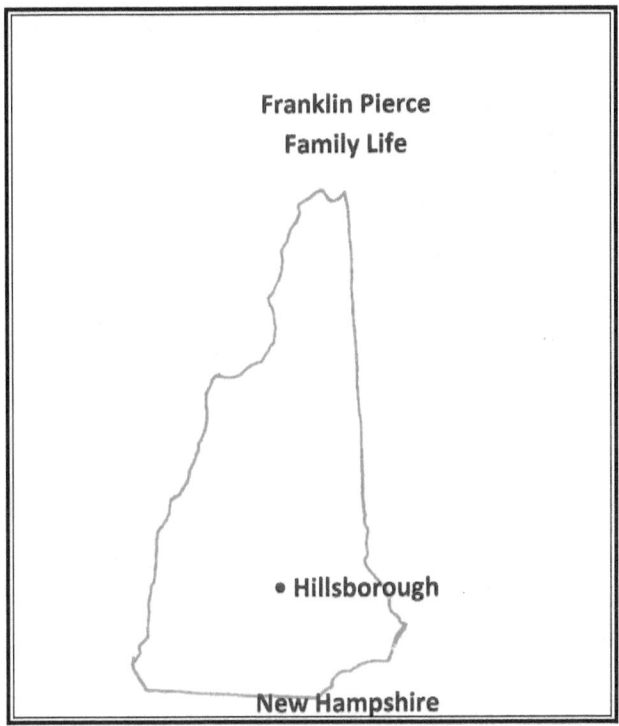

Franklin Pierce
Family Life

• Hillsborough

New Hampshire

Franklin Pierce was born in Hillsboro, New Hampshire on November 23, 1804. His father was Benjamin Pierce, a farmer and former Governor of New Hampshire. His mother was Anna B. Kendrick, a distant cousin of first lady, Barbara Bush. He was the fifth of eight children. In 1824, he attended Bowdoin College in Maine and graduated third in his class. He became a lawyer and began a practice in Concord, New Hampshire. Pierce married Jane Means Appleton the daughter of Bowdoin College President, Jesse Appleton. They lived permanently in Concord, New Hampshire where they had three children, all of whom died in childhood.

**James Buchanan, 15th President, 1856-1860:** James Buchanan was born in Mercersburg, Pennsylvania in 1791. He is the only president to remain a lifelong bachelor.

He served in the U.S. House; and, when the Federalist Party was disbanded, he was elected to the Senate as a Democrat. He resigned from the Senate to become James K. Polk's Secretary of State where he helped negotiate the 1846 Oregon Treaty. with Britain establishing the 49$^{th}$ parallel as the northern boundary between the western United States and Canada.

Buchanan ran for the Democratic presidential nomination in 1852 but lost to Franklin Pierce who made him Minister to Great Britain. Buchanan won the Democratic nomination in 1856 and beat the Republican nominee, James Fremont of California. This was the first time that a Democrat and Republican opposed each other establishing a precedent that has endured ever since..

The Democrats wanted to preserve the Union while the Republicans were anti-slavery. In 1857, Congress rejected the pro-slavery Constitution of Kansas. In 1858, Northern anti-slavery candidates won a majority in both houses of Congress. The conflicting viewpoints of Congress and President Buchanan prevented any significant legislation from being passed. South Carolina seceded from the Union followed by six other southern states

Modern Day Contemporary: There is no modern day person that has had to deal with a divided country like what plagued Buchanan.

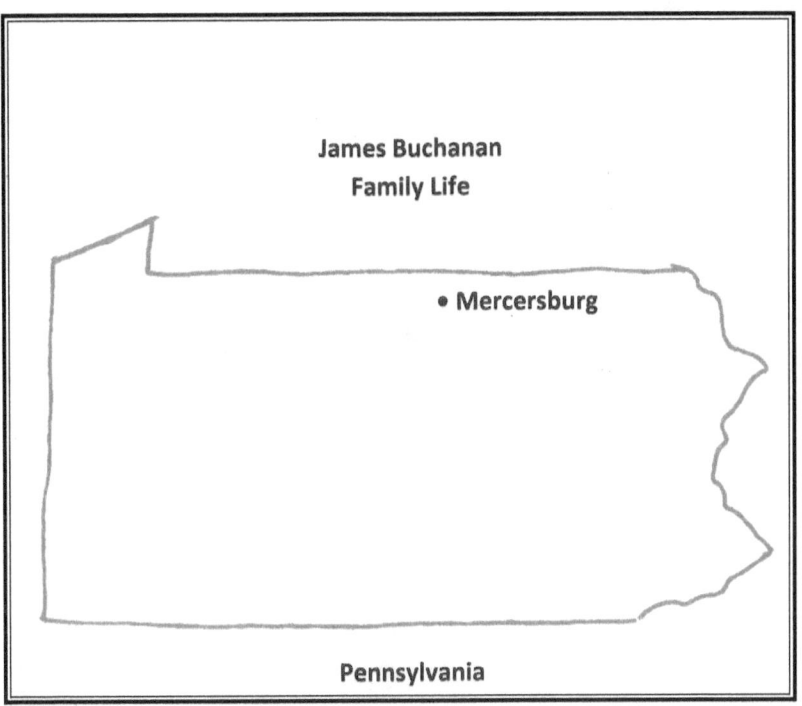

James Buchanan was born in Mercersburg, Pennsylvania on April 23, 1791. His father was James Buchanan Sr. from Ireland and his mother was Elizabeth Speer Buchanan. James was second in a family of eleven children. He attended Dickinson College graduating in 1809. He was engaged once but never married. His support of Andrew Jackson gave him a road to the Presidency.

# Minnesota and Oregon Entered the Union 1858-1859

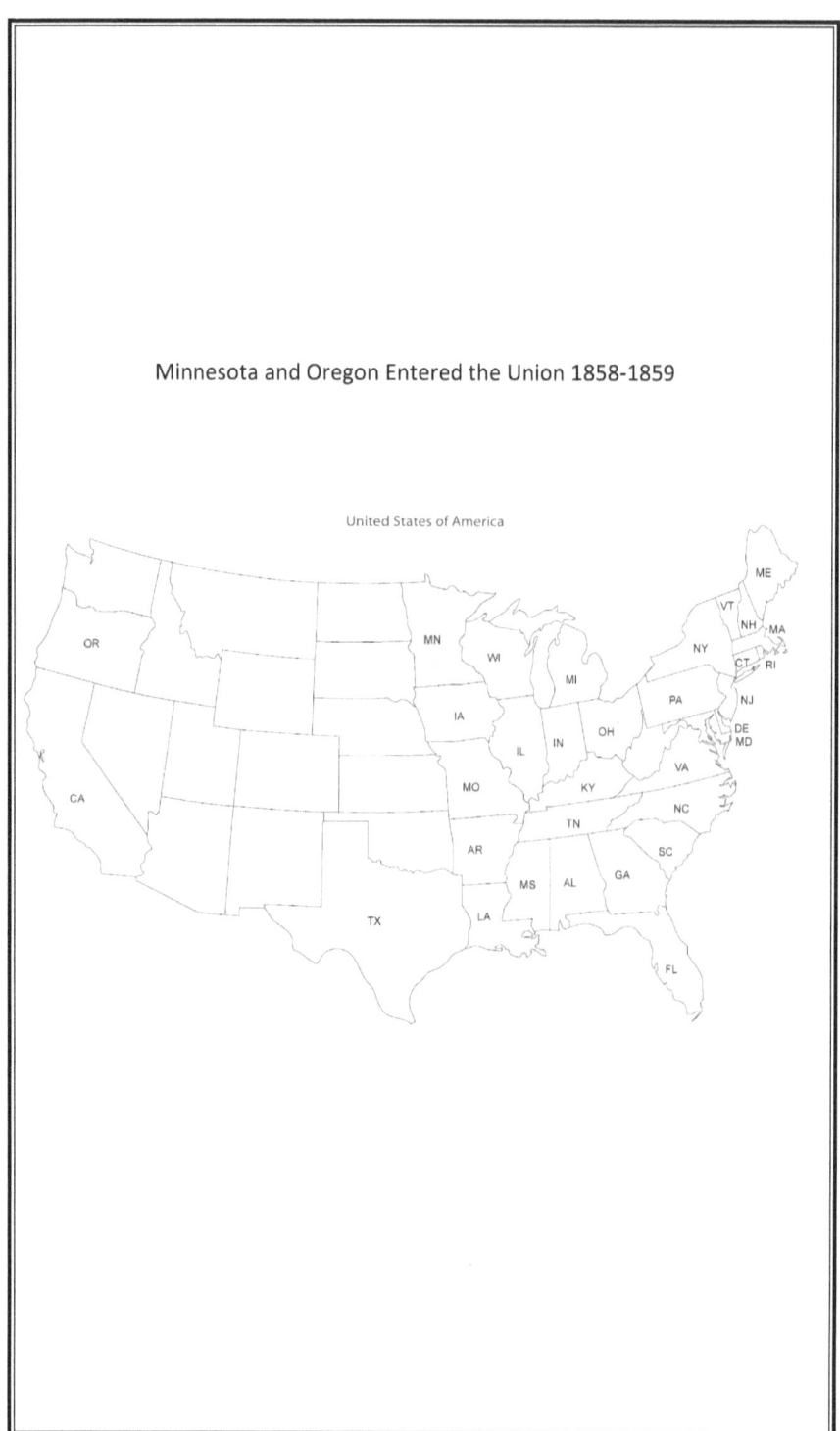

United States of America

**Abraham Lincoln, 16th President, 1860-1865:** Lincoln was born in Hardin County, Kentucky; grew up in Indiana; and, settled in Illinois. He became a lawyer and was elected to the U.S. House where he became a nationally known figure.

Abraham Lincoln was president during a tragic moment in American history. The Civil War broke out between the North and the South threatening to divide the Union. The war lasted four years in which 24 major battles were fought. One million men were killed or wounded; far more than any other war in U.S. history.

In 1856, Lincoln joined the anti-slavery Republican Party after the Whig Party disbanded. In 1860, he was nominated for president by the Republican Party. He beat southern Democrat John Breckinridge. South Carolina and six other southern states seceded from the Union just before Lincoln was inaugurated. After the inauguration, the Civil War broke out when South Carolina fired on the U.S. base at Fort Sumter.

Early Southern victories discouraged Lincoln; however, in the election year of 1864, the war turned in favor of the North. Lincoln won the election by beating Democrat George B. McClellan, a former Union Army General.

On April 9, 1865, while watching a play at Ford's Theatre in Washington, Lincoln was shot by John Wilkes Booth. Booth, from Maryland, was a well-known actor and Confederate sympathizer. On April 15, Lincoln died and Vice-President Andrew Johnson took office.

Modern Day Contemporary: Abraham Lincoln was a great president who has no modern day peer.

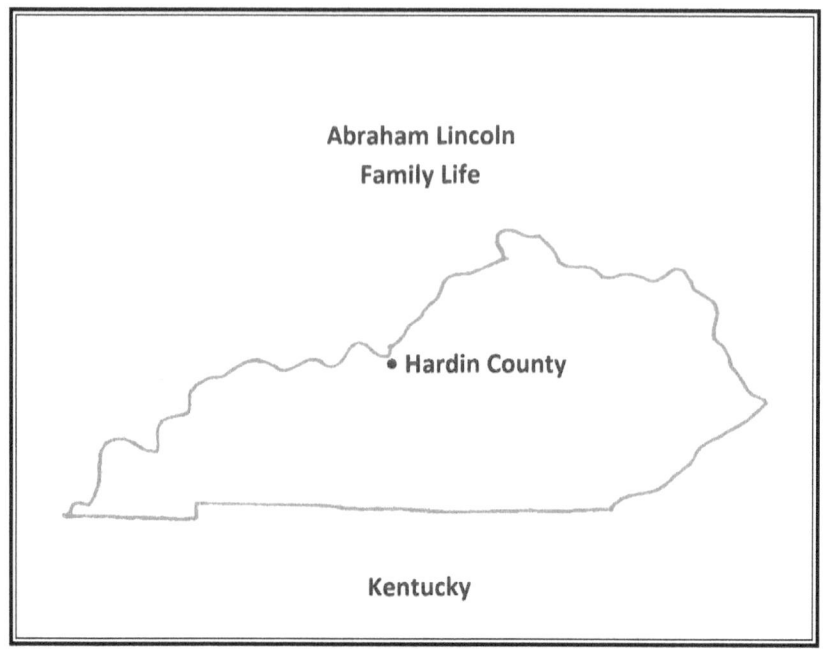

Abraham Lincoln
Family Life

• Hardin County

Kentucky

Abraham Lincoln was born in Hardin, now Larue County, Kentucky. His father, Thomas Lincoln, a woodworker, migrated from Virginia. His mother was Nancy Hanks Lincoln. They had three children, one dying in infancy. Abraham was born on February 12, 1809. In 1816, the Lincoln's moved to Indiana where Lincoln grew up in frontier country. In 1830, the Lincoln's moved to near Decatur, Illinois. Lincoln settled in New Salem, Illinois where he served in the army during the Black Hawk War. In 1834, he was elected to the Illinois General Assembly. He became a lawyer and moved to the capital, Springfield, Illinois in 1837. There he met Mary Todd whom he married on November 4, 1842. They had four sons with only one, Robert Todd Lincoln, living to adulthood.

# Kansas, West Virginia, Nevada & Nebraska

## Entered the Union 1861-1867

United States of America

**Andrew Johnson, 17th President, 1865-1868:** Vice-President Johnson took over the top office when Lincoln was assassinated. Johnson was the first president to be impeached; however, the Senate failed by one vote to remove him from office.

Andrew Johnson was born in Raleigh, North Carolina; but, grew up in Tennessee. He was elected to the U.S House. He became governor of Tennessee and then U.S. Senator when slavery was the main issue of the day. He tried to steer a middle path. When the Southern states started to secede, he tried to keep Tennessee in the Union. Johnson was the only senator not to secede with his state.

In 1864, the Republican Party made Democrat Johnson the Vice-Presidential candidate under Lincoln. After Lincoln's assassination, Johnson kept Lincoln's cabinet and tried to follow his policy of rebuilding the South without dealing severe punishment; however, radical members of Congress wanted to punish the South and put them under military rule. The House voted the necessary two-thirds majority to impeach Johnson. The most important reasons given were that he violated the Tenure of Office Act and that he conspired against Congress. The Tenure Act was passed in 1867 and prevented Johnson from dismissing any officials whose appointment was approved by the Senate. He tried to dismiss Secretary of War Stanton to test the Act; but, was unsuccessful. The conspiracy charge was made because he said that Congress did not properly represent all the states. On May 16, 1868, the Senate missed by one vote to have Johnson removed from office. In the election of 1868, Johnson campaigned for the democratic presidential nomination; but, instead it went to Governor Horatio Seymour of New York.

Modern Day Contemporary: President Clinton is the only other president to be impeached; however, he was impeached for different reasons and is not considered a contemporary of Johnson.

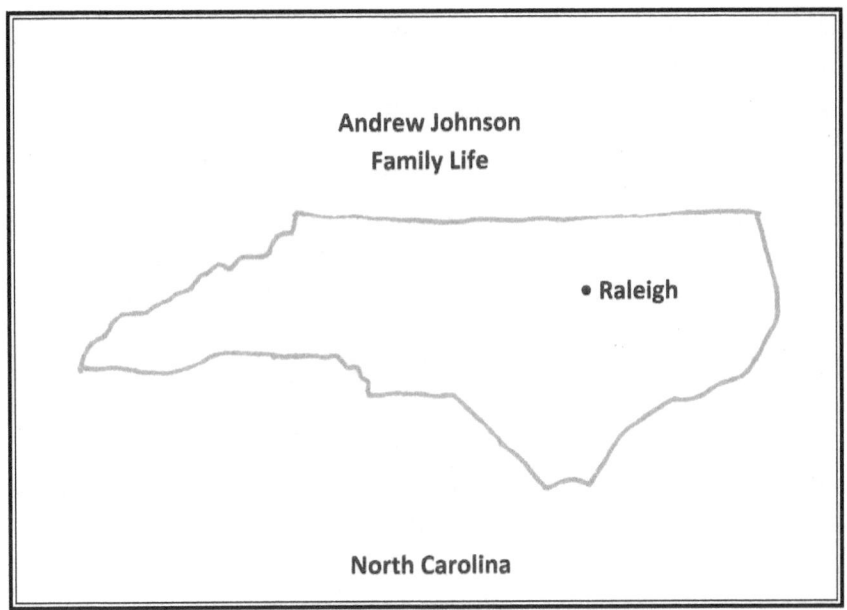

Andrew Johnson
Family Life

• Raleigh

North Carolina

Andrew Johnson was born on December 29, 1808 in Raleigh, North Carolina. His father was Jacob Johnson and his mother was Mary McDonough Johnson. Andrew was the younger of two sons. His father died when Andrew was just three years old. Andrew became a tailor and settled in South Carolina. In 1825, he brought his mother, stepfather, and older brother to Tennessee with him. On May 17, 1827, Johnson married Eliza McCardle. They had five children. Johnson was greatly influenced by the beliefs of fellow Tennessean, Andrew Jackson.

**Ulysses S. Grant, 18th President, 1868-1876:** Ulysses S. Grant was a successful Civil War general who was made Commander of all Union Forces. Grant's success on the battlefield took him to the White House.

Ulysses Grant was born in Point Pleasant, Ohio and graduated from West Point. He fought in the Mexican War and resided in Missouri and Illinois. He volunteered for the Civil War; and, in 1861, was promoted General of the Army. He was successful in winning battles down the Mississippi Valley while other Union forces in the East were losing. President Lincoln once said, "I can't spare this man – he fights." He was made Commander of all Union forces in the West; and, in 1864, was made Commander of the entire Union Army. Grant captured the Confederate capital Richmond; and, in 1865, accepted General Lee's surrender. Grant became very popular in the North and the people of the South appreciated the kind treatment he gave Lee's men.

In the election of 1868, the Republican Party nominated Grant for president. He defeated Democrat Horatio Seymour who was a former Governor of New York. Grant tried to limit the number of federal troops in the South and tried to bring the North and South together. He was denied by Congress to create a Civil Service Commission to try to curb corruption in government. In 1871, he arranged the Treaty of Washington with Great Britain. The United States was paid $15,500,000 because Great Britain built ships for the South during the war that destroyed much of the North's fleet. Grant was reelected in 1872 over Democrat Horace Greeley, editor of the New York Tribune. In 1873, several eastern banks failed and hard times hit the South and West. Congress passed an $18,000,000 currency inflation bill which Grant vetoed. Several important government officials were accused of wrong doing in office. Despite this, many Republican leaders wanted to nominate Grant for a third term. He refused and Ohio Governor Rutherford B. Hayes got the nomination.

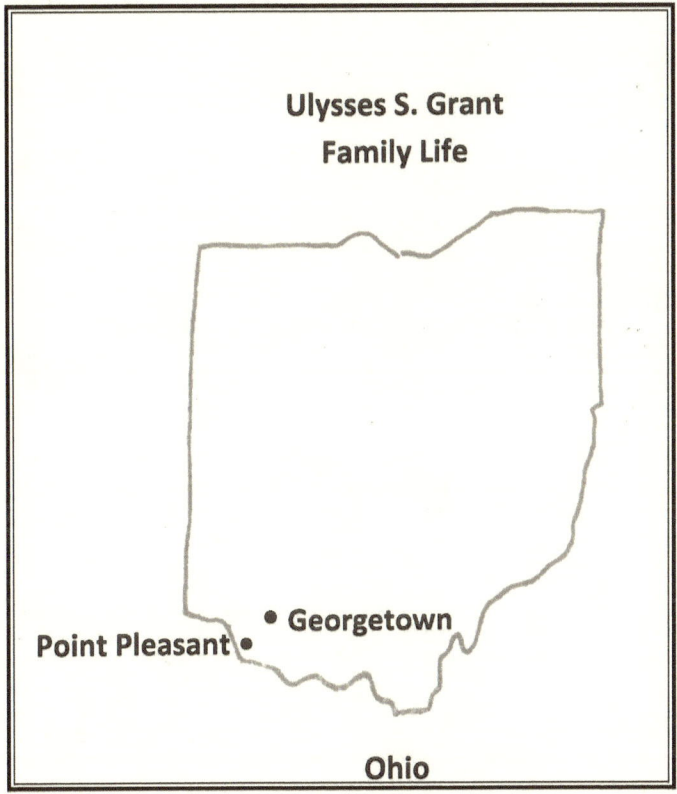

Ulysses S. Grant
Family Life

Point Pleasant •  • Georgetown

Ohio

On April 27, 1822, U.S. Grant was born in Point Pleasant, Ohio to Jesse and Hannah Simpson Grant. He was the eldest child and, a year later, the family moved to Georgetown, Ohio. There were two more brothers and three sisters born in Georgetown. In 1829, Ulysses entered West Point where he ranked high in mathematics and horsemanship. He graduated and was stationed near St. Louis. He took part in the capture of Mexico City and was praised for bravery. He returned to St. Louis and married Julia Denton August 22, 1848. They had four children. Grant was sent out west on assignment but became lonely, resigned from the army, and returned to St. Louis to be with his family. Grant was 39 years old when the Civil War broke out.

Colorado Entered the Union as the 38<sup>th</sup> State in 1876

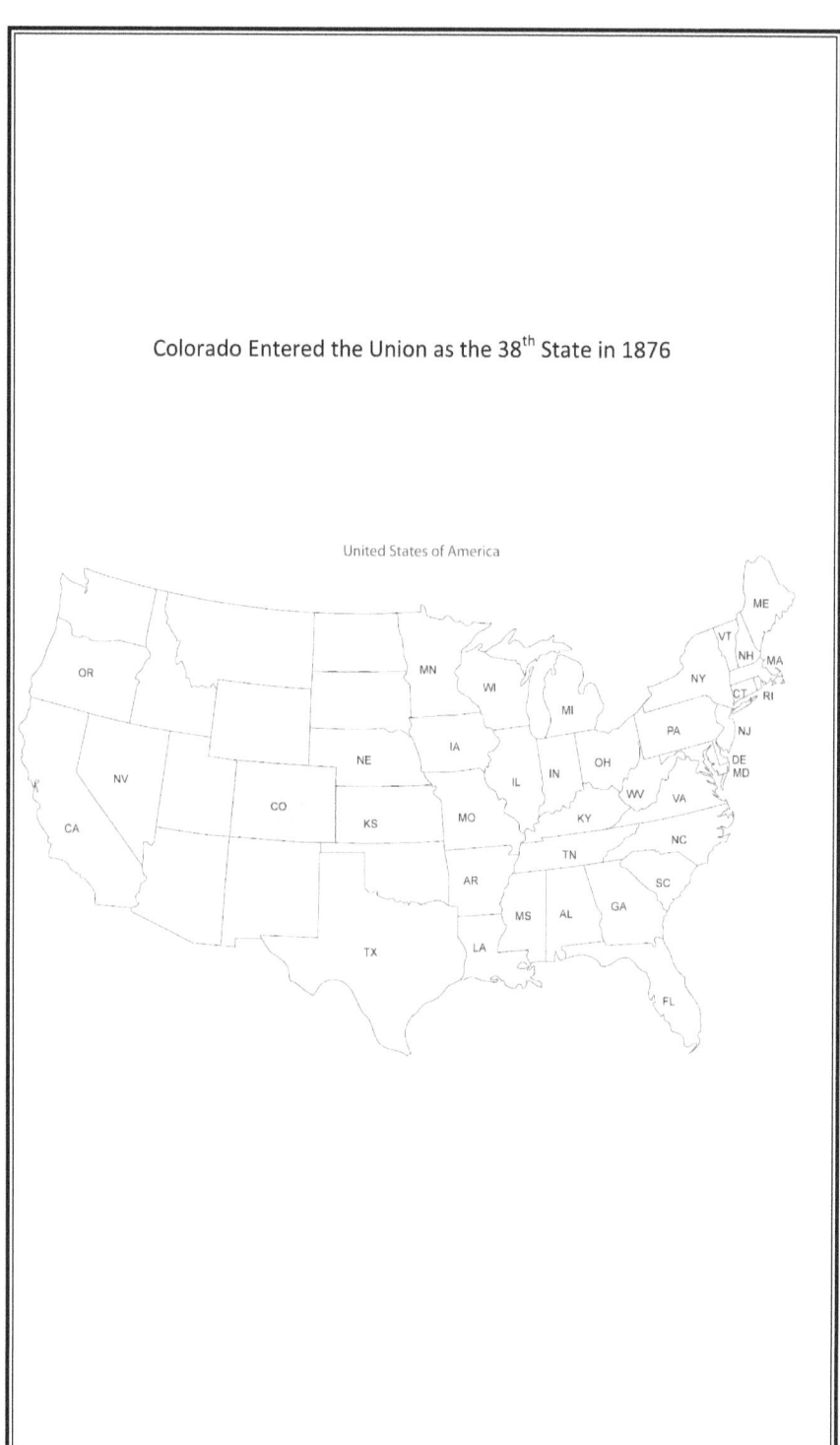

United States of America

**Rutherford B. Hayes, 19th President, 1876-1880:** Rutherford B. Hayes won the presidency by only one electoral vote. Because of disputed electoral votes from Florida, Louisiana, Oregon, and South Carolina, Congress appointed an electoral commission. The commission agreed by the Electoral College decision giving the presidency to Hayes by a vote of 185 to 184 over Samuel Tilden.

Hayes was born in Delaware, Ohio and went to Kenyon College. He attended the Harvard Law School and began practicing law in Fremont, Ohio. Hayes wife was the former Lucy Ware Webb of Chillicothe, Ohio. She was a graduate of the Wesleyan Female College of Cincinnati and the first president's wife to have a college degree.

Hayes moved his practice to Cincinnati where he joined a group of Ohio volunteers who fought in the Civil War. Hayes fought bravely and was wounded four times. After the war, he resigned as a General.

Hayes was elected to the U.S. Senate and then Governor of Ohio. He worked for economy in government; a strong Civil Service Commission based on merit; and, he helped to establish the Ohio State University.

In 1876, Hayes was the Republican presidential nominee beating Samuel Tilden, Governor of New York. In office, one of the first things he did was to remove all Federal troops out of the South. He announced that he would run for just one term as President. He did this so he could make political appointments based on merit rather than to political friends. Hayes proposed Civil Service legislation, but Congress refused to act. His fight became popular and encouraged future presidents to support the policy. Secretary of the Treasury John Sherman helped to restore financial confidence by offering gold for paper money which was issued to help finance the Civil War.

**Rutherford B. Hayes**
**Family Life**

• **Delaware**

**Ohio**

Rutherford B. Hayes was born in Delaware Ohio on October 4, 1822 to Rutherford and Sophia Birchard Hayes. He was the fifth child but only he and his sister Fanny grew to adulthood. His father died two months before Rutherford was born. He graduated at the head of his class from Kenyon College in Ohio. He graduated from the Harvard Law School and was admitted to the bar in 1845. He opened up a law office in Cincinnati and became a famous trial lawyer. He married Lucy Ware Webb on December 30, 1852. They had eight children with only five living to adulthood. Hayes served in the Civil War and was wounded four times. After the war Hayes resigned from the army with the rank of Major General. He became a three times governor of Ohio and helped establish the Ohio State University.

**James A. Garfield, 20th President, 1880-1881:** James A. Garfield was born in Orange Township (near Cleveland), Ohio, and the third straight president to be born in Ohio. He was the second president to be assassinated and the fourth to die in office. He was shot by Charles Guiteau who was angry because he didn't get an appointment to the American Consul in Paris. (Guiteau was tried and hanged in 1882.) Garfield died 80 days later and was replaced by Vice-President Chester A. Arthur of New York.

Garfield attended Hiram College where, at the age of 26, was made president of the college. After the start of the Civil War, he was commissioned an officer in the Ohio Volunteers. He was made a General, the youngest in the Union Army, after he won a battle in Kentucky. He took part in the Battle of Shiloh and distinguished himself in the Battle of Chickamauga.

Garfield was elected to the U.S. House where he served as Chairman of the Appropriations Committee. He served on the commission that declared the 1876 Presidential election winner to be Rutherford B. Hayes. He was elected the Republican Presidential nominee on the 36th ballot because delegates couldn't make up their minds between favorite James Blaine from Maine and former President Ulysses S. Grant. Garfield went on to defeat Democrat Winfield Scott Hancock, a former Union Army General.

Garfield spent his short time in office appointing his supporters government jobs. The Spoils System was still in effect and thousands of people lost their jobs every time a new president was put into office. Garfield predicted that Civil Service reform would be enacted because of the tremendous waste of presidential time with the Spoils System. Two years later, the Pendleton Civil Service Act was passed ending the Spoils System of appointing government jobs.

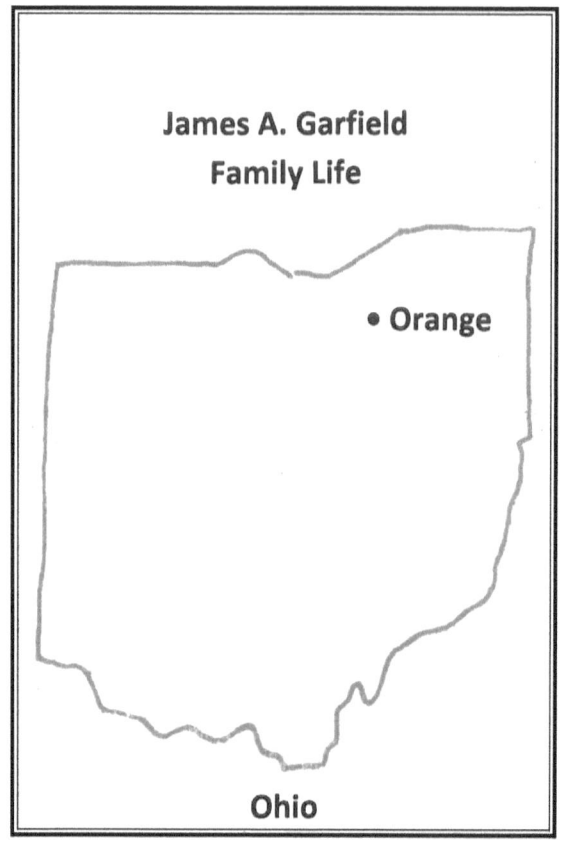

**James A. Garfield
Family Life**

• Orange

**Ohio**

James A. Garfield was born in Orange, Ohio, (near Cleveland) on November 19, 1831. His parents were Abram and Eliza Ballou Garfield. James was the fifth born of five children. James father died when he was only two years old leaving his mother to manage a thirty acre farm. He graduated from Williams College in Williams, Massachusetts in 1856. He was made President of Hiram College, Hiram Ohio at the age of 26. He married Lucretia Rudolph on November 11, 1858. They had seven children, two of them dying in infancy. Son Harry Augustus Garfield became President of Williams College and was a member of President Woodrow Wilson's administration during World War I. Another served in President Theodore Roosevelt's administration. During the Civil War, Garfield was made a Major General for heroism in action.

**Chester A. Arthur, 21st President, 1881-1884:** Chester A. Arthur was the fourth vice-president to be sworn into the top office after the death of the president. Arthur was born in Fairfield, Vermont and practiced law in New York City. He became a general in the New York Militia during the Civil War.

In the Republican convention of 1880, Arthur was made the vice-presidential candidate to run with James Garfield of Ohio. Garfield beat Democrat Winfield Scott Hancock, a former Union Army General. Garfield was shot in July, 1881, and died two months later.

Arthur became president; and, a year later learned that he was dying of kidney (Bright's) disease. Because of the assassination of President Arthur by a turned-down government job seeker, there was public sentiment to end the Spoils System of giving government jobs to political supporters.

In 1883, Congress passed the Pendleton Civil Service Act which based government hiring on merit rather than political party. Arthur tried to reduce import tariffs to help American consumers but, Congress ignored a commission report. The U.S. Navy was modernized under Arthur's initiative.

In the Republican convention of 1884, Arthur was beaten by former Secretary of State, James Blaine for the presidential nomination. Blaine was beaten by Democrat Grover Cleveland in the national election. Arthur resumed his law practice in New York City. He died of kidney disease in 1886. He had kept his illness a secret.

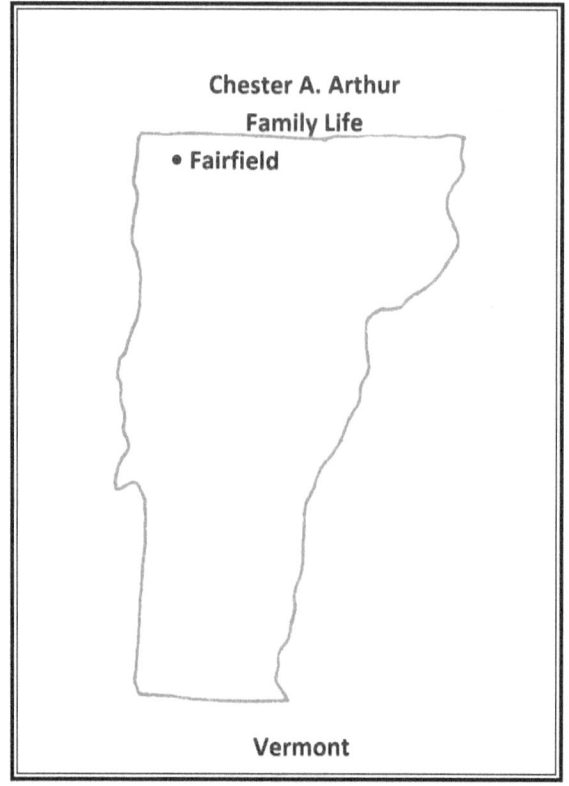

Chester A. Arthur was born on October 3, 1829, in Fairfield, Vermont, the first son in a family of six girls and three boys. His father William came from Northern Ireland. His mother, Malvina Stone Arthur, was raised on a farm in Vermont. He graduated from Union College in Schenectady, New York at the age of eighteen. He became a lawyer and joined a New York City law firm. He married Ellen Lewis Herndon, on October 31, 1859, the daughter of a navy officer. They had two sons and a daughter. The older boy died at a young age. Mrs. Arthur died a year later leaving Chester to raise Chester Jr. and Ellen.

**Grover Cleveland, 22nd President, 1884-1888:** Grover Cleveland is the only man to serve two non-consecutive terms as President. He beat Republican James Blaine of New York in the election of 1884. He lost to Republican Benjamin Harrison in 1888 and then beat Harrison in the election of 1892.

Grover Cleveland was born in Caldwell, New Jersey and became a lawyer in Buffalo. He worked his way up in the Democrat Party and was elected Governor of New York. Cleveland was made the Democratic presidential nominee in 1884. He ran against James Blaine who was a former Secretary of State. The Democrats had not been able to elect a president since James Buchanan in 1856. Cleveland won the election by only 23,005 votes.

As president, Cleveland made his cabinet members run honest and efficient departments. The railroads were made to return to the government vast tracts of land that were never used. Labor riots in Chicago prompted Cleveland to propose a government arbitration board. He wanted lower tariffs because the government was taking in more money than it was spending and he wanted farmers in the South and West to spend less for imported goods. New silver mines were opening and the metal was being sold to the government at a 1 to 16 ratio to gold. Because the Treasury was being drained of all its gold, Cleveland wanted to go to a gold standard; but, Congress refused.

Cleveland was the first president to be married in the White House. He was 49 when he married 21 year old Frances Folsom, daughter of his former law firm partner. Cleveland lost the 1888 election to Republican Benjamin Harrison even though he had 90,728 more popular votes. In 1892, Cleveland was again elected beating Harrison 271 votes to 145.

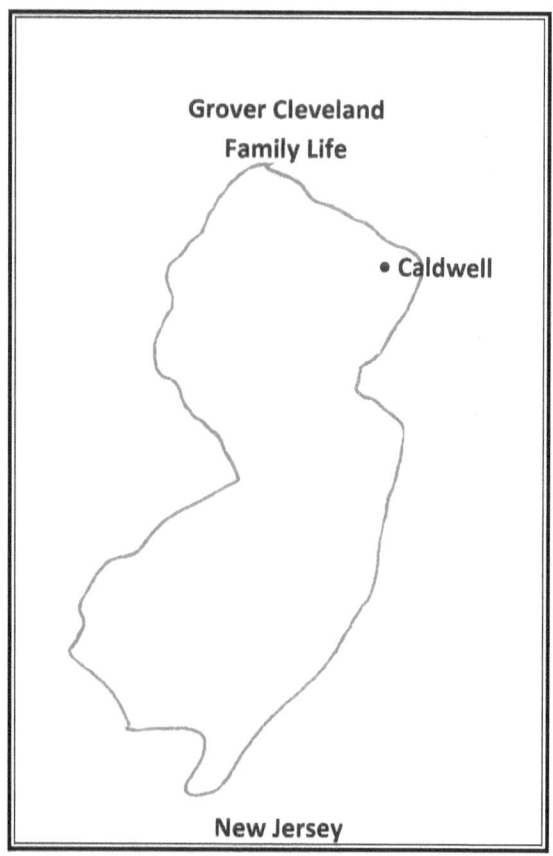

Steven Grover Cleveland was born in Caldwell, New Jersey on March 18, 1837 to Robert Falley and Ann Neal Cleveland. He was a relative of the founder of the city of Cleveland, Ohio. He was the fifth child of a family of nine. He became a lawyer in Buffalo, New York in 1859. He became mayor of Buffalo and then governor of New York in 1882. Cleveland married Frances Folsom in the White House in June, 1886. The Cleveland's had five children with Ester Cleveland being the only one to be born in the White House.

**Benjamin Harrison, 23rd President, 1888-1892:** Benjamin Harrison was the fourth president to be born in Ohio and the only grandson of a president to take the high office. His father was John Scott Harrison who was the son of the 9th president, William Henry Harrison.

Benjamin Harrison was born in North Bend, Ohio and graduated from Miami University, Oxford, Ohio. He became a lawyer and moved to Indianapolis, Indiana. He fought many battles in the Civil War and was made a General. In 1881, he was elected to the U.S. Senate where he fought for Civil Service reform, a protective tariff, a strong Navy, and regulation of the railroads.

The Republicans nominated Harrison for president in 1888. He beat incumbent Democrat Grover Cleveland. Harrison received 90,728 fewer votes than Cleveland, but won the electoral vote count 233 to 168.

The Sherman Anti-Trust Act was passed during Harrison's term of office. It outlawed large trusts from preventing competition and controlling the price of goods. The Sherman Silver Purchase Act was also passed. It increased the amount of silver that could be coined. Because the government gave gold for some silver purchases, fear of a drain on the Treasury helped fuel a financial panic in 1893. The McKinley Tariff Act raised tariffs to record heights. This increased prices and forced the cost-of-living up.

In the election of 1892, Harrison lost to Democrat Grover Cleveland, the man he beat in 1888. Harrison won by 372,735 popular votes but lost by an electoral vote count of 277 to 145.

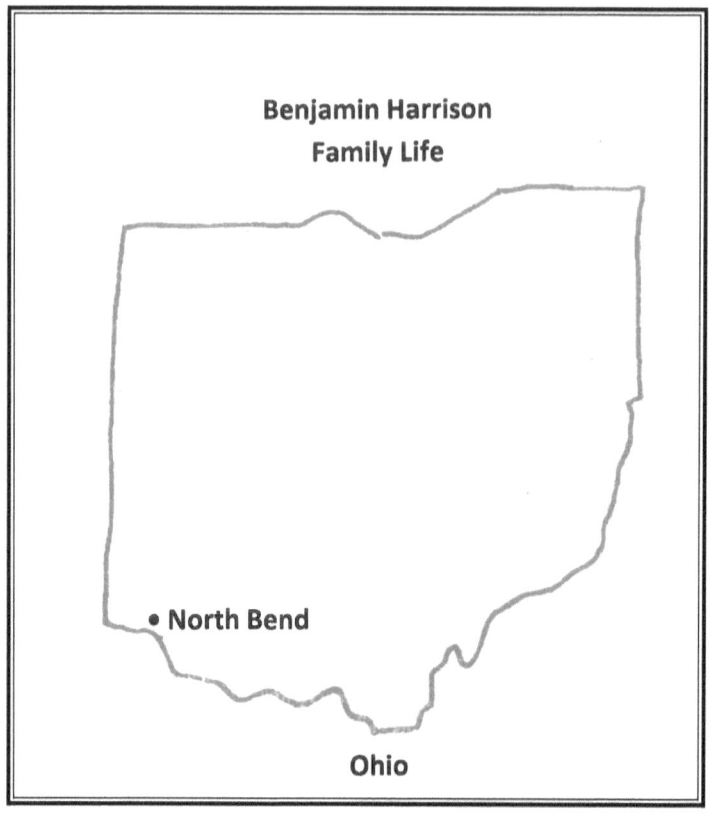

**Benjamin Harrison Family Life**

• **North Bend**

**Ohio**

Benjamin Harrison was born on a farm in North Bend, Ohio on August 20, 1833. His great grandfather, having the same name, was a signer of the Declaration of Independence. He was the second of ten children born to his parents, John Scott and Elizabeth Irwin Harrison. He graduated from Miami University, Oxford, Ohio in 1852 and married Caroline Lavinia Scott in 1853. They had two children, Russell Benjamin and Mary. In 1854 Harrison was admitted to the bar and moved to Indianapolis. He fought in the Civil War where he rose to the rank of brigadier general.

# North & South Dakota, Montana, Washington, Idaho & Wyoming

## Entered the Union 1889-1890

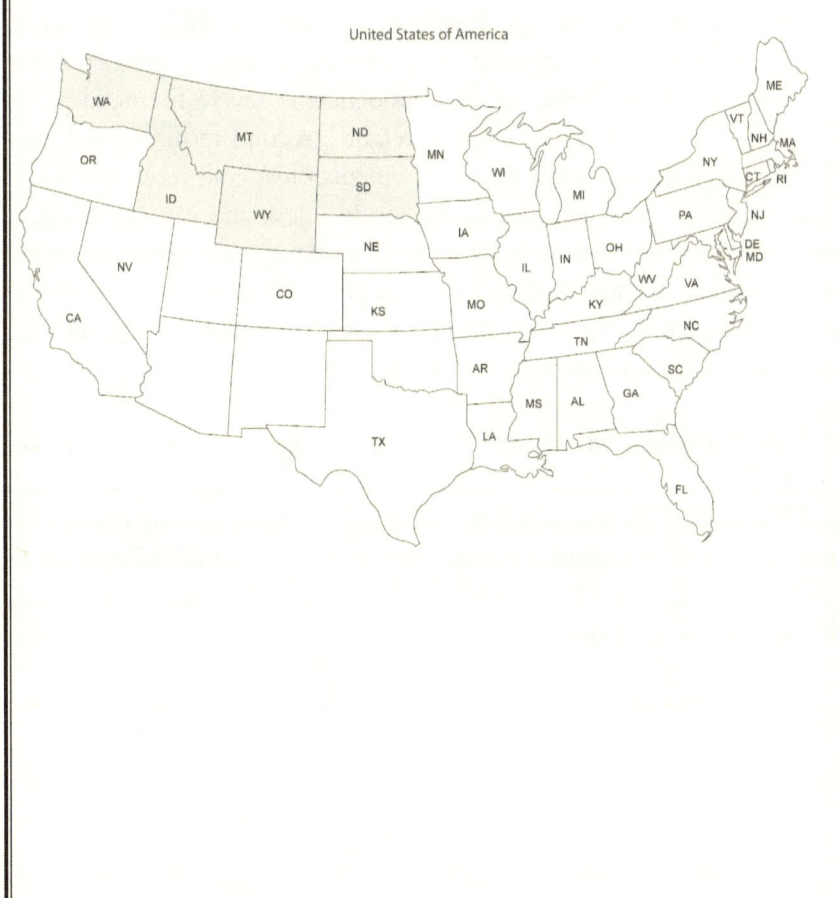

United States of America

**Grover Cleveland, 24th President, 1892-1896:** Grover Cleveland, the 24th President, was also the 22nd President. In his initial attempt at the presidency, he beat Republican James Blaine of Maine. He then lost to Benjamin Harrison in 1888 and beat Harrison in 1892. Grover Cleveland was born in Caldwell, New Jersey and became a lawyer in Buffalo. He worked his way up in the Democrat ladder and became Governor of New York. He was elected Democratic presidential nominee in 1884 when he beat James Blaine who was a former Secretary of State. The Democrats had not been able to elect a president since James Buchanan in 1856. Cleveland lost the 1888 election to Republican Benjamin Harrison even though he had 90,728 more votes. The electoral vote count was 233 for Harrison and 168 for Cleveland.

Before becoming president, Cleveland had moved to New York City and resumed his law practice. President Harrison favored higher tariffs and increased purchases of silver. Cleveland criticized Harrison's policies and, in 1892, was elected to the presidency. A severe financial panic hit the country in 1893 during Cleveland's second term as president. The Treasury floated bond issues to replenish lost gold reserves. When Eastern bankers bought most of the bonds, Cleveland was criticized. It was during this time that he was found to have cancer of the mouth. His upper left jaw was replaced with an artificial rubber piece that was hardly noticeable. The news was kept a secret because of the nation's financial condition, but it eventually leaked out.

In 1894, Cleveland sent federal troops to Chicago to break up a railroad strike. He intervened in a boundary dispute between Great Britain and Venezuela. Cleveland's popularity had hit a low during his second term. He actually favored the monetary policies of the 1896 Republican candidate William McKinley over his own Democratic candidate, William Jennings Bryan.

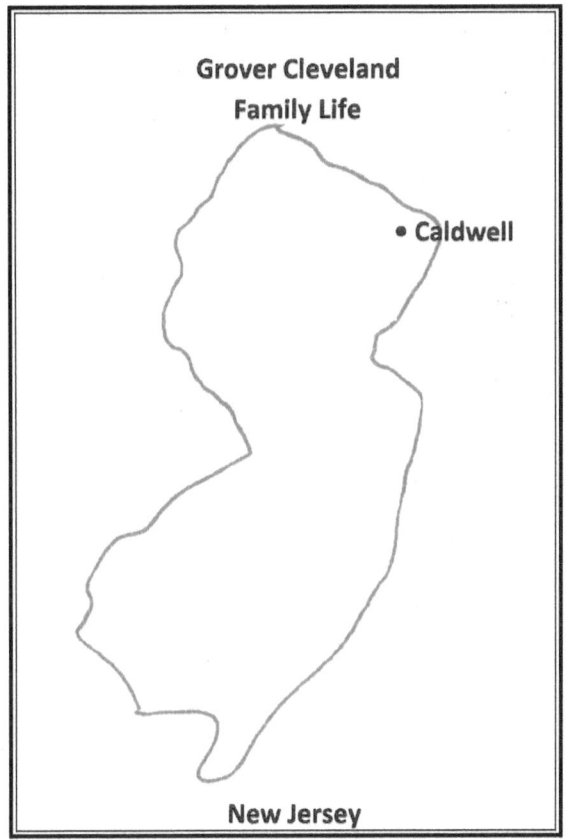

Steven Grover Cleveland was born in Caldwell, New Jersey on March 18, 1837 to Robert Falley and Ann Neal Cleveland. He was a relative of the founder of the city of Cleveland, Ohio. He was the fifth child of a family of nine. He became a lawyer in Buffalo, New York in 1859. He became mayor of Buffalo and then governor of New York in 1882. Cleveland married Frances Folsom in the White House in June, 1886. The Cleveland's had five children with Ester Cleveland being the only child to be born in the White House.

**William McKinley, 25th President, 1896-1901:** William McKinley was the fifth president born in Ohio. He was president during the Spanish-American War in which the United States fought Spain over the independence of Cuba.

William McKinley was born in Niles, Ohio and was the first man in his town to volunteer for the Civil War. By the end of the war, he had become a major. After the war, he studied law and began his career in Canton, Ohio. In 1876, he was elected to the U.S. Senate where he supported high tariffs to help U.S. businesses against foreign competition. He was elected Governor of Ohio; and, in 1896, won the Republican nomination for President. He beat William Jennings Bryan, a newspaperman from Nebraska by an electoral vote count of 271 to176.

As promised in his campaign, McKinley raised tariffs to all-time highs. Congress passed the Gold Standard Act of 1900 to back paper money. On April 25th, 1898, after the U.S. battleship Maine blew up in the Havana, Cuba harbor, the U.S. declared war on Spain. A revolution had been going on in Cuba for two years. The war lasted only 113 days. Cuba was granted independence and the U.S. received Guam, the Philippines, and Puerto Rico.

In the election of 1900, the Democrats again elected Bryan as their presidential nominee. McKinley won by an even greater electoral vote count of 292 to 155.

On September 5, 1901, at the Pan-American Exposition in Buffalo, New York, McKinley made a speech indicating that he had changed his position on high tariffs because of a surplus of U.S. manufactured goods. The next day at a public reception, a man named Czolgosz went up to shake McKinley's hand and shot him. Czolgosz said that he had an urge to kill a great leader. McKinley died eight days later. Vice-President Theodore Roosevelt, one of the heroes of the Spanish-American War was sworn in the same day. Czolgosz was tried and electrocuted.

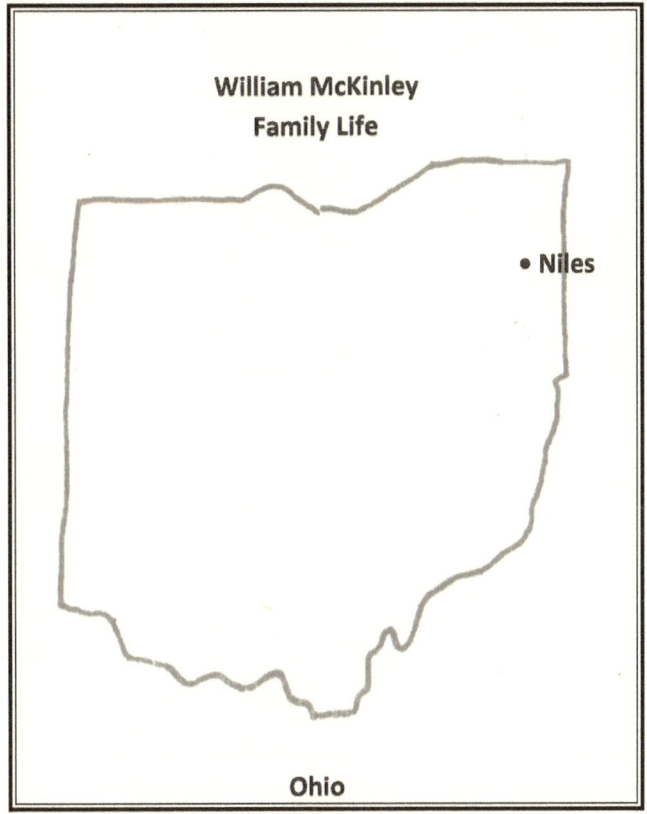

**William McKinley Family Life**

• **Niles**

**Ohio**

On January 29, 1843, William McKinley was born in Niles, Ohio to William and Nancy Allison McKinley. He fought in the Civil War and was promoted to major. He studied law; was admitted to the bar in 1867 and, practiced law in Canton, Ohio. He married Ida Saxton on January 25, 1871. They had two daughters, one dying at age four months and the other at four years. Mrs. McKinley became an invalid the rest of her life. McKinley looked after and was devoted to her throughout his career.

Utah Entered the Union as the 45<sup>th</sup> State in 1896

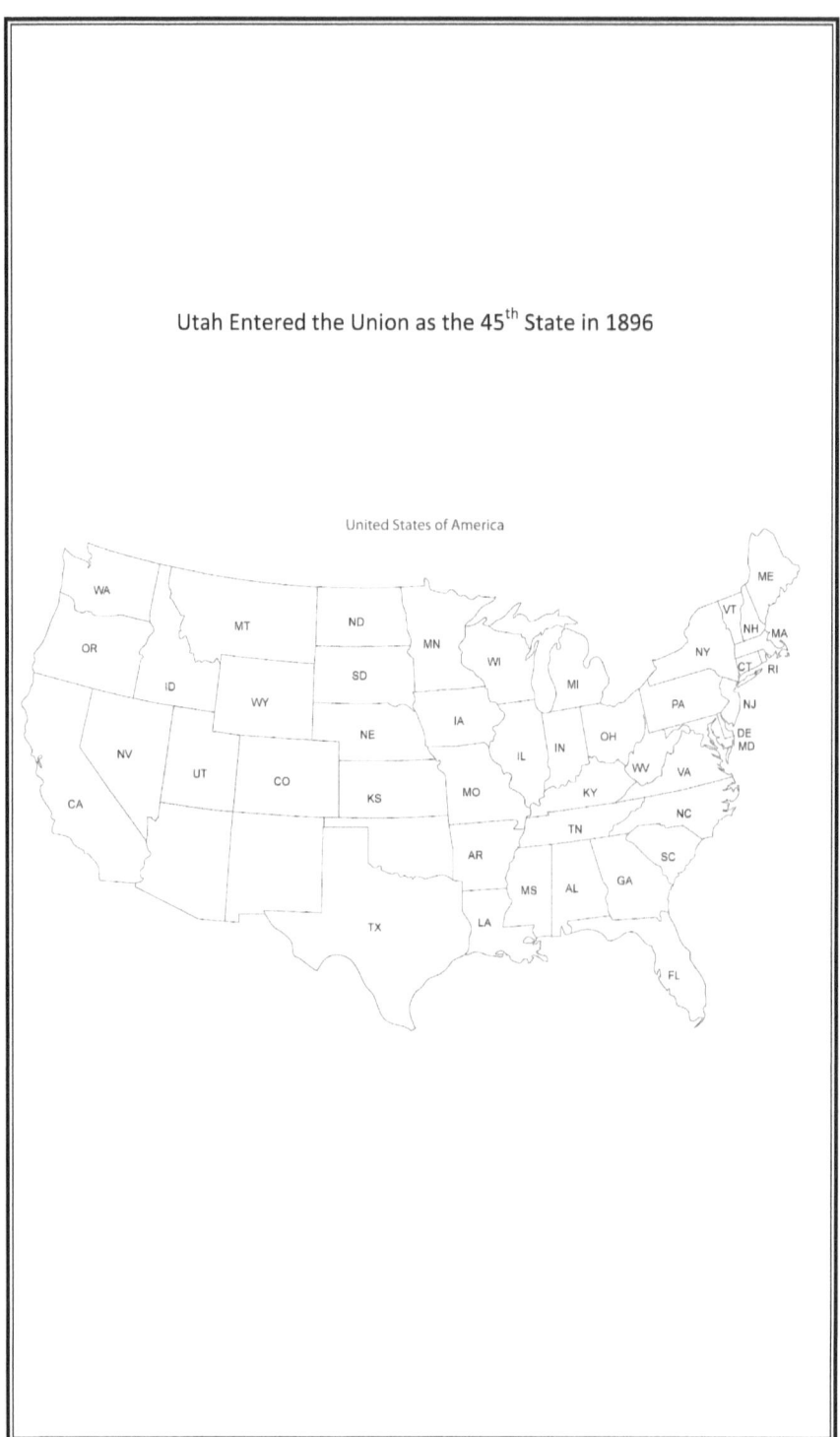

United States of America

**Theodore Roosevelt, 26th President, 1901-1908:** Theodore Roosevelt was vice-president 6 months when President William McKinley was shot and died 8 days later. Roosevelt was sworn in and led the nation with much vim and vigor. After he left office, he said; "I do not believe that anyone else has ever enjoyed the White House as much as I."

Roosevelt was born in New York City and graduated from Harvard University. In 1884, after the death of his wife and mother, he ran two ranches in the Dakota Territory. In 1888, President Benjamin Harrison appointed him to the Civil Service Commission. President McKinley made him Assistant Secretary of the Navy.

When the Spanish-American War broke out, Roosevelt resigned his government position so he could join the fight. He led a group of cavalry in the Battle of San Juan Hill in Cuba and became nationally famous.

In 1898, Roosevelt was elected Governor of New York; and, in two years, was elected the Vice-Presidential candidate to run with Republican William McKinley. They defeated Democrat William Jennings Bryan; but, after McKinley's assassination, Roosevelt was made the youngest chief executive ever at age 42.

One of his first accomplishments was to break up big corporation monopolies. John D. Rockefeller's oil and J.P. Morgan's railroad companies were two of the victims. Roosevelt had built up the Navy and he wanted a canal to shorten the route between the Atlantic and Pacific Oceans. In 1903, he negotiated unsuccessfully with Columbia for a strip of land in their province of Panama. When Panama rebelled against Columbia, Roosevelt sent in troops. A treaty was quickly signed with Panama to build the canal which was completed in 1914; Roosevelt's greatest achievement.

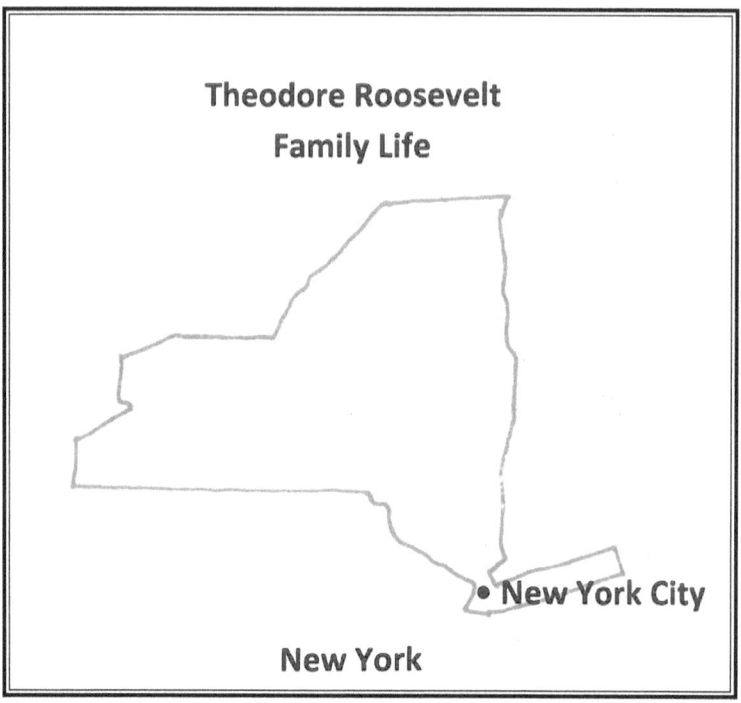

Theodore Roosevelt was born in New York City on October 27, 1858 to Theodore and Martha Bulloch Roosevelt. He was second of four children. The Roosevelt's are related to a Dutch family that came over from Holland in the 1640's. Theodore's mother came from Georgia and sympathized with the South during the Civil War. Roosevelt graduated from Harvard in 1880. He was married in October, 1879 to Alice Hathaway Lee, the daughter of a wealthy member of a Boston investment firm. Alice died on February 14, 1884 two days after the birth of a daughter, who was also named Alice. That same day, Roosevelt's mother died. In 1884, Roosevelt bought two cattle ranches in the Dakota Territory. He returned to New York in 1886 after severe winters in the West destroyed his cattle. Roosevelt married a childhood friend, Edith Kermit Carow, on December 2, 1886. They had five children. After being the Assistant Secretary of the Navy, Roosevelt became a national hero for gallantry in action in the Spanish-American War in Cuba.

# Oklahoma Entered the Union as the 46<sup>th</sup> State in 1907

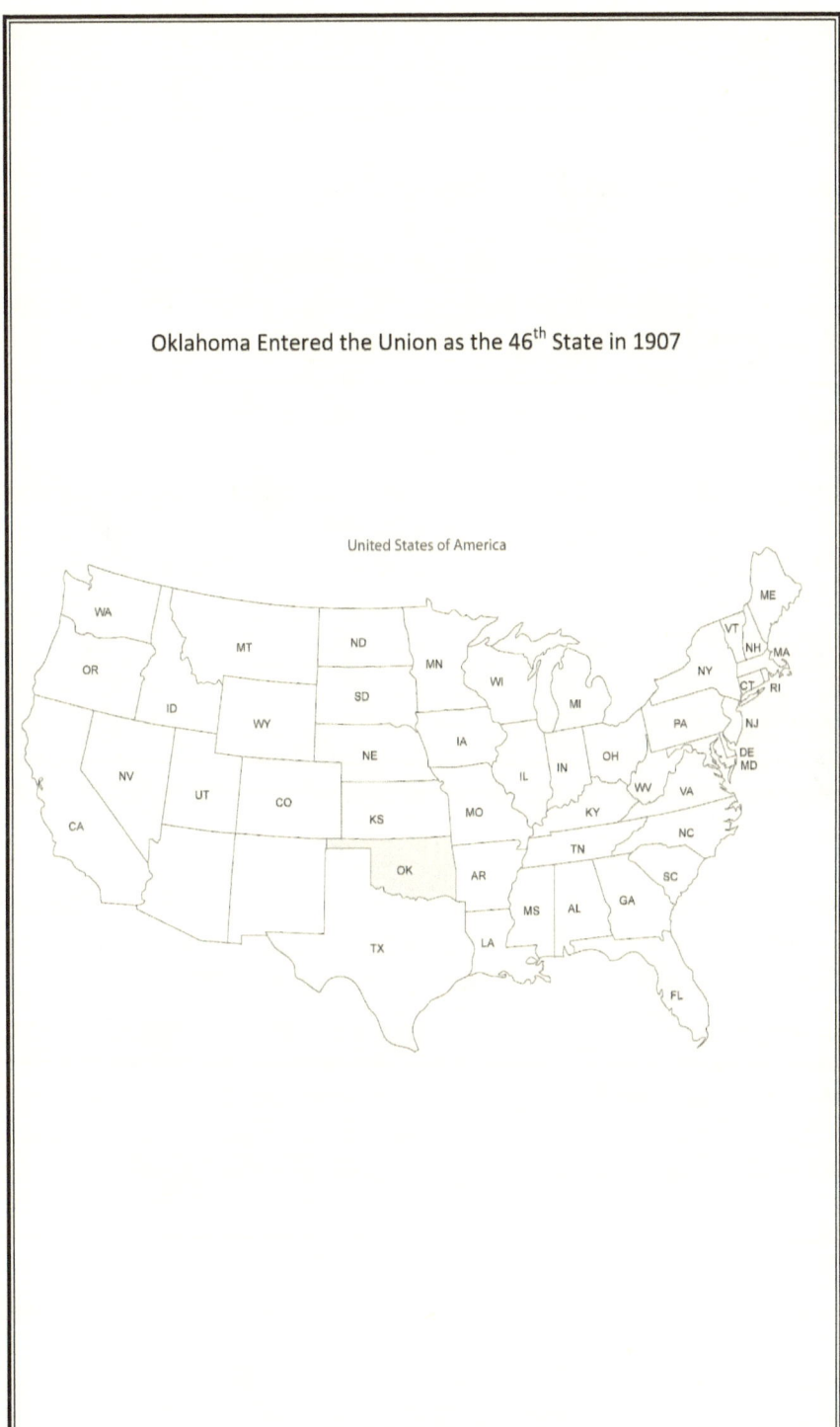

United States of America

## William Howard Taft, 27th President, 1908-1912: William
Howard Taft was the sixth president to be born in Ohio. His mother
was happy with him being a judge. His father and wife wanted him in
politics. In 1908, when President Theodore Roosevelt chose not to run
again, he recommended Taft who won easily.

Taft was born in Cincinnati, Ohio and graduated from Yale. He became
a lawyer like his father Alphonso Taft who was well known in the
Republican Party. In 1890, Taft was appointed Solicitor General of
the U.S. by President Benjamin Harrison. President Harrison then
made him an Appeals Court judge. In 1901, he became the first civil
governor of the Philippines where he did an admirable job of improving
living conditions. He gained popularity for his efforts and later, became
Secretary of War under Roosevelt. In 1908, Roosevelt chose not to
run again and selected Taft as his successor. Taft easily beat Democrat
William Jennings Bryan by an electoral vote of 321 to 162. Taft's
legislative program was hampered by a badly split Republican Party. He
did push a bill through forcing federal election candidates to publish
campaign expenses. He prosecuted twice as many "trust busting" cases
as his predecessor. He was the first to ask his cabinet members for a list
of predicted campaign expenses which developed into today's federal
budget.

In 1912, the Republican Party chose Taft to run again. He was beaten
badly by Woodrow Wilson who had 435 electoral votes for only 8 for
Taft. Theodore Roosevelt, surprisingly, ran under the Progressive Party
name, and garnered 88 electoral votes, badly splitting the Republican
vote. Taft was elected President of the American Bar Association in 1913.
In 1921, President Harding made him Chief Justice of the Supreme
Court. Taft said it was the highest honor of his life. He and John F.
Kennedy are the only two presidents buried in the Arlington National
Cemetery in Virginia.

**William Howard Taft**
**Family Life**

• Cincinnati

Ohio

William Howard Taft was born in Cincinnati, Ohio on September 15, 1857 to Alphonso and Louise Maria Torrey Taft. Both Taft and his wife's families had migrated from England to New England. Taft's father was a successful Cincinnati lawyer and a nationally known Republican figure. Taft had two younger brothers and a sister and two older step brothers. In 1878, He graduated second in his class from Yale College. He received his law degree in 1880 and practiced in Cincinnati. He married Helen Herron on June 19, 1886. They had three children; Robert who became a famous Republican Senator; Helen who became a dean at Bryn College in Pennsylvania; and Charles who was mayor of Cincinnati. Taft held many Ohio state and national offices before he became president.

**Woodrow Wilson, 28th President, 1912-1920:** Woodrow Wilson was born in Staunton, Virginia; the seventh president to be born in Virginia. He was a scholar and a man of peace. He served as president during World War I.

Woodrow Wilson graduated from Princeton, and received a PhD from Johns Hopkins. He became the Democratic Governor of Virginia; and, in 1912, the Democratic Presidential Candidate. He won the national election with 435 electoral votes against 88 for Progressive candidate Theodore Roosevelt, and only 8 for incumbent Republican William Howard Taft. Wilson, working with a Democratic Congress, passed legislation establishing lower tariffs, the Federal Reserve System, the Federal Trade Commission, and the 8 hour work week. He narrowly averted war in deposing Mexican dictator Victoriano Huerta. He then sent General John J. Pershing into Mexico to stop the border raids of bandit Poncho Villa. In August 1914, World War I broke out in Europe; and, in 1915, a German submarine sank the British passenger liner Lusitania killing 128 Americans. Wilson fought to remain neutral and barely won the election of 1916 receiving 277 electoral votes to 254 for Republican Supreme Court Justice Charles Hughes.

When German submarines began attacking American ships, Wilson urged Congress to go to war. The United States entered the war in the fourth and final year helping Britain, France, Russia, and Italy beat Germany, Austria-Hungary, and Bulgaria. Wilson fought for a League of Nations as part of the peace treaty but the Senate failed to ratify the bill. In the election of 1920, Republican Warren G. Harding who rejected the League of Nations beat Democrat James Cox.

Wilson suffered a stroke in 1919 and served out his term as an invalid. After the presidency, he formed a law firm in Washington. He died in his sleep in 1924 and was buried in the Washington Cathedral, the only president to be buried in Washington D.C.

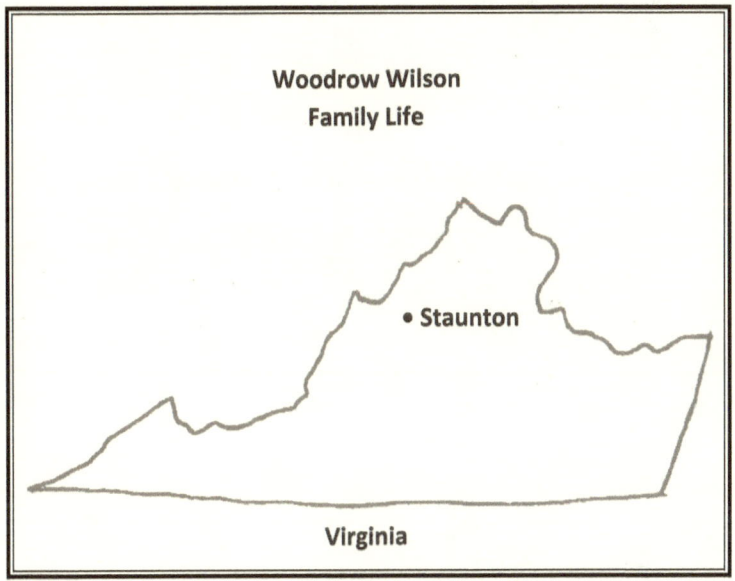

Woodrow Wilson
Family Life

• Staunton

Virginia

Woodrow Wilson was born in Staunton, Virginia on December 29, 1856 to Joseph Ruggles and Janet Woodrow Wilson. He was the third in a family of four children. Wilson's father was a minister so his youth was full of religion and learning. He graduated from Princeton in 1879. Wilson became a lawyer and then received a doctorate degree from Johns Hopkins in June 1886. He married Ellen Louise Axson on June 24, 1885. The Wilson's had three daughters. Wilson became a college professor and was made president of Princeton University. He was elected governor of New Jersey which propelled him to the presidency.

New Mexico and Arizona, the last two Contiguous States,

Entered the Union in 1912

United States of America

Alaska and Hawaii, the last two States, entered the Union in 1959

**Warren G Harding, 29th President, 1920-1923:** Warren G. Harding was the seventh president born in Ohio and the sixth president to die in office. He died in the fourth year of his presidency from what was thought to be pneumonia while on a speaking trip out West.

Harding was born in Blooming Grove, Ohio and graduated from Ohio Central College. He became a newspaper owner in Marion, Ohio. In 1914, he was elected to the U.S. Senate. Harding enjoyed the Senate but was persuaded to run for the presidency by his wife. In the 1920 Republican convention, he was elected the presidential candidate when the delegates couldn't agree on Frank Lowden of Illinois, General Leonard Wood, or Senator Hiram Johnson of California. Harding campaigned against the United States joining the League of Nations and to return to the normalcy of pre-World War I days. Harding beat James Cox, Governor of Ohio, by an electoral vote count of 404 to 127.

Harding quickly signed World War I peace treaties which did not contain the League of Nations provisions that former President Woodrow Wilson desired. In 1921, Congress imposed quotas on immigration for the first time; and, in 1922, tariffs were raised to record levels. Secretary of the Interior Albert Fall was eventually sent to prison for what was called the "Teapot Dome" scandal. He was convicted of taking bribes for government oil reserves. A depression hit the farm belt in 1921 and the Republicans lost heavily in the Congressional elections of 1922. Harding went on a western speaking trip to try to regain confidence of the populous. He became ill in what doctors in San Francisco diagnosed as pneumonia. He died in 1923 before fulfilling his term of office and was buried in Marion, Ohio. Vice-President Calvin Coolidge took the oath of office finishing the term.

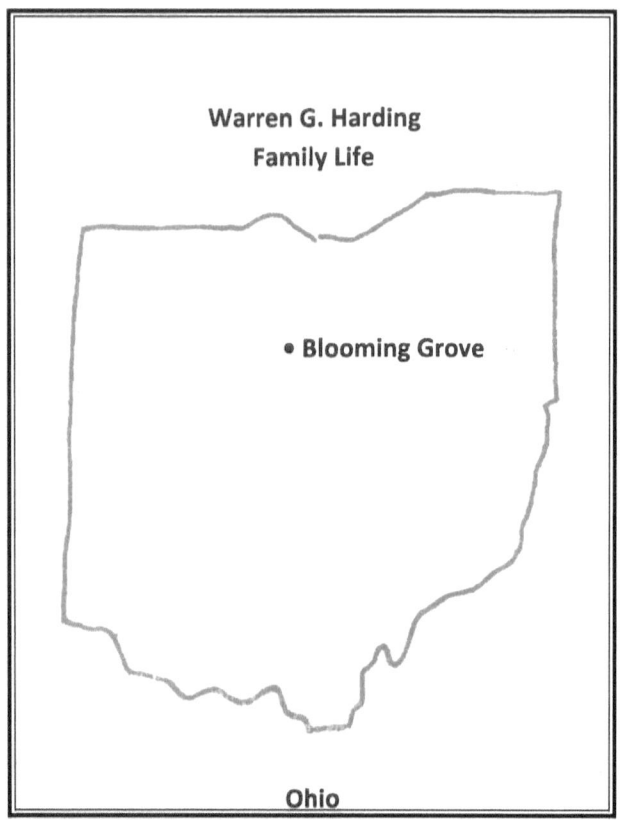

Warren G. Harding was born on a farm near Blooming Grove, Ohio on November 2, 1865 to George Tyron and Phoebe Dickerson Harding. His parents moved to Marion, Ohio in 1882 where he later taught school and purchased an interest in the local newspaper. In 1881, Warren married divorcee Florence Kling DeWolfe who helped her husband in his political career. They had no children. Harding was senator then lieutenant governor of Ohio before losing the election for governor. Warren ran successfully for the U.S. Senate in 1914 where he became nationally known in his rise to the presidency.

**Calvin Coolidge, 30th President, 1923-1928:** Calvin Coolidge was the sixth vice-president to take the high office after the death of the president. Coolidge was a quiet man who served the country during the "roaring twenties". He enjoyed great popularity and probably could have served another term had he chose to run.

Coolidge was born near Woodstock, Vermont and graduated from Amherst College. He moved to Massachusetts where he became a lawyer and was elected Governor. He was the Republican Vice-President to Warren Harding in 1920. When Harding died in 1923, Coolidge was sworn in as President. He reached the White House just as the Teapot Dome and other scandals involving the Harding administration surfaced. He forced the resignation of Attorney General Harry Daugherty and other officials implicated in the scandals. Coolidge continued Harding's policies of supporting business.

In the election of 1924, Coolidge beat Democrat John Davis, former ambassador to Great Britain by an electoral vote count of 382 to 136. The Harding administration scandals had not hurt Coolidge. The country was prosperous and the people loved this quiet, conservative man. Secretary of State Frank Kellogg helped draft the Kellogg Peace Pact which was signed by most nations of the world condemning war. Kellogg won the 1929 Nobel Peace Prize for his efforts. Coolidge opposed joining The League of Nations, but he wanted to join the World Court. Vice-President Charles Dawes led an international committee that worked out a plan for Germany to pay its World War I debt.

Coolidge chose not to run in 1928 because of the pressures of the office on himself and his wife. On October, 1929, shortly after his term expired, the stock market crashed. Coolidge felt he was partly to blame and died of a heart attack in 1933.

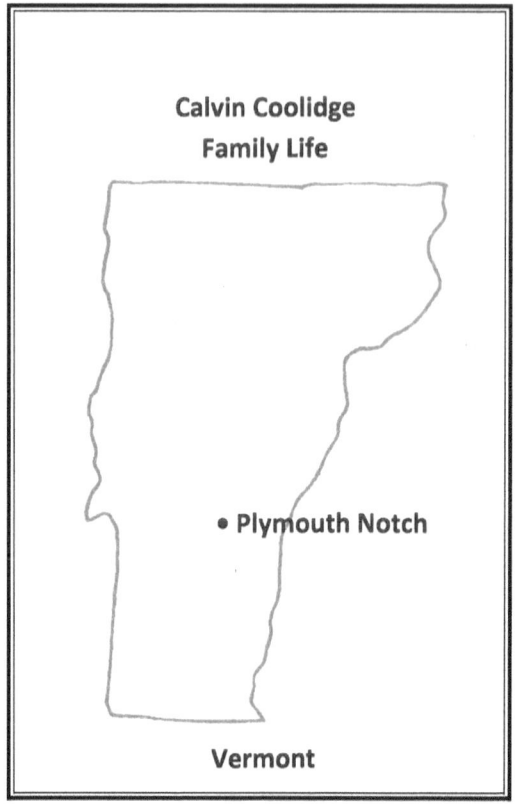

Calvin Coolidge was born in Plymouth Notch, Vermont on July 4, 1872 to John Calvin and Victoria Josephine Moor Coolidge. He attended two academies and then Amherst College where he graduated cum laude in 1895. In 1897, he became a lawyer in Massachusetts and opened up his own office in Northampton. He married his wife, Grace Anna Goodhue on October 4, 1905. They had two sons, John and Calvin junior. Calvin senior worked his way up the political ladder in Massachusetts ending up being elected governor three times giving him the recognition he needed to be elected U.S. Vice-President.

**Herbert Hoover, 31st President, 1928-1932:** Herbert Hoover was the first president born west of the Mississippi River. He was in office when the Great Depression hit the country. He was the first president to use the resources of the government to fight a depression.

Hoover was born in West Branch, Iowa and graduated from Stanford University with a degree in mining engineering. He worked as a mining engineer in California, Australia, and China. He started his own company in London where he organized a "Food for Europe" program in World War I under President Wilson. He became Secretary of Commerce for both Presidents Harding and Coolidge.

Hoover was the Republican candidate for president in 1928 beating Democrat Al Smith, Governor of New York, by a record vote of 444 to 87. Smith wanted to repeal the law banning the sale of alcoholic beverages while Hoover fought against it. In October 1929, seven months after Hoover took office, the stock market crashed. Many people lost their jobs and businesses failed. Congress and Hoover passed laws to loan money to businesses to prevent bankruptcy. Money was also sent to states for relief to laid-off workers. Public works and conservation jobs were started including the Hoover Dam.

When the depression would not end, many people wanted a change in Washington. In the election of 1932, Frank D. Roosevelt, Governor of New York, beat Hoover by an electoral vote count of 427 to 59.

After World War II, President Truman sent Hoover to Europe to study the food needs of the nations. In 1947, The Hoover Commission found ways to streamline and cut cost in government. Hoover gave all his income from government service to charity. He died in 1947 in New York City at the age of 90. He was buried in West Branch, Iowa.

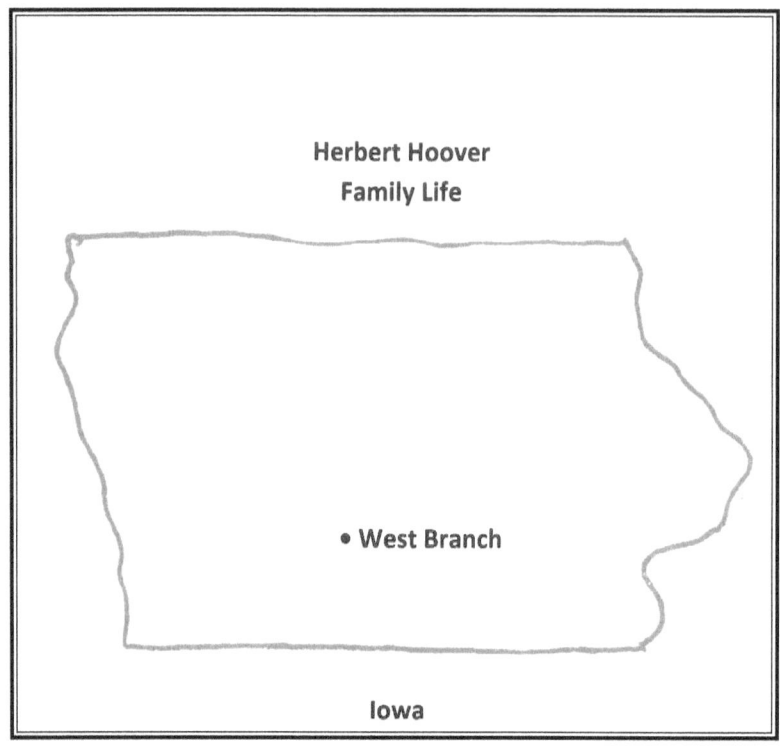

**Herbert Hoover
Family Life**

• **West Branch**

**Iowa**

Herbert Hoover was born in West Branch, Iowa on August 10, 1874 to Jesse Clark and Huldah Randall Minthorn Hoover. Herbert had an older brother Theodore and a younger sister May. Hoover's parents both died when he was young and was raised by relatives. He moved out west to live with an uncle and, in 1895, graduated from Stanford University as a mining engineer. There he met Lou Henry. He married her on February 10, 1899 in Monterey, California. They had two sons, Herbert junior, who also became a mining engineer, and Allan, who became director of a mining company. Hoover developed mines in countries all around the world. He organized relief efforts for the people of Europe during World War I. This made him an internationally known figure leading him to the White House.

## Franklin Delano Roosevelt, 32nd President, 1932-1945:

Franklin Delano was elected to the presidency four terms, far more than any other individual. He had to cope with the Great Depression and World War II while in office.

Roosevelt was born in Hyde Park, New York, the fifth cousin of former president, Theodore Roosevelt. He graduated from Harvard and married his distant cousin Eleanor Roosevelt. He was made Secretary of the Navy. In 1920, he was the democratic candidate for vice-president. Shortly after, he contacted polio and had to wear leg braces the rest of his life. He was elected Governor of New York; and, four years later, beat Herbert Hoover for the presidency by an electoral vote count of 472 to 59. The country was in the midst of the Great Depression and Roosevelt had campaigned to help citizens cope through the hard times. Roosevelt and Congress pushed through many programs to provide jobs and relief for the unemployed elevating the national debt to record levels.

In 1936, Roosevelt beat Alfred Landon, Governor of Kansas by a record electoral vote count of 523 to 8, losing only the states of Maine and Vermont. Germany invaded Poland in 1939. In the election of 1940, Roosevelt won a record third term beating Wendell Willkie, who was a corporate president from Indiana by a vote of 449 to 82. In December of 1941, Japan attacked Pearl Harbor. A day later, the U.S. declared war on Japan. Three days after that, Germany and Italy declared war on the U.S., with the U.S. reciprocating on the same day. November 1942, the Allies invaded North Africa and in 1944, the Allies landed on Normandy.

In the election of 1944, Roosevelt, whose health was stating to fail, beat Thomas E. Dewey by a vote of 432 to 99. In April 1945, Roosevelt died of a cerebral hemorrhage in Warm Springs, Georgia. He was buried in Hyde Park. In May 1945, Germany surrendered followed by Japan three months later.

**Franklin Delano Roosevelt**
**Family Life**

● Hyde Park

**New York**

Franklin Delano Roosevelt was born on January 30, 1882 in Hyde Park, New York to James and Sara Roosevelt. His parents were both wealthy and he was an only child. He had a well-guided up-bringing and was taught to care for those who were not as fortunate as himself. In 1903, Franklin graduated from Harvard; and, in 1904 entered Columbia University Law School. He passed the bar exam but had no enthusiasm for becoming a lawyer. Franklin married his distant cousin, Eleanor Roosevelt on March 17, 1905. They had six children, two of them, James and Franklin Jr. serving in the U.S. House of Representatives. Roosevelt did not enter the military service but toured Europe during World War I and became a nationally known figure. On August 2, 1921, Roosevelt fell in the water off Campobello Island in New Brunswick, Canada. He became ill and contacted polio. He had to wear leg braces the rest of his life.

**Harry S. Truman, 33rd President, 1945-1952:** Harry Truman took the oath of office on April 12, 1945, the day that Franklin Roosevelt died. Roosevelt had served only 83 days of his record fourth term. On May 7, Germany surrendered. Truman approved dropping an atomic bomb on Hiroshima on August 6 and on Nagasaki August 9. Japan surrendered on August 14. After the war, Russia took over the nations of Eastern Europe. The Truman Doctrine gave aid to the nations of Western Europe to fight Communism. The Marshall Plan helped the nations of Western Europe rebuild.

Democrat Truman, from Lamar, Missouri, won the 1948 presidential election upsetting Republican Thomas Dewey of New York. In 1949, the U.S. and Canada joined with the nations of Western Europe to form NATO, the North Atlantic Treaty Organization, to defend Western Europe. On June 25, 1950, North Korea crossed the 38th parallel to invade South Korea. Two days later, Truman ordered U.S. forces to aid South Korea. That same day, the U.N. approved sending troops to aid in the same cause. By September, the North Koreans had captured all of South Korea except a small area of land on the southeastern tip around the city of Pusan. On September 16, General Douglas MacArthur directed an amphibious landing at Inchon on the west central coast of South Korea near the 38th parallel. The capital Seoul which was 24 miles inland was captured on September 26. By October, the North Koreans were driven close to the Chinese border. On October 25, China entered the war and, by January 1951, had pushed the U.N. forces back across the 38th parallel. By July, 1953, after bitter fighting for many hills, the U.N. forces drove the communist forces just north of the 38th parallel where a truce line was established.

Truman did not seek reelection in 1952. He retired to Independence, Missouri where his friends built the Harry S. Truman Library. He died on December 26, 1972 after suffering lung congestion and was buried in the Library Courtyard.

Harry S. Truman was born in Lamar, Missouri on May 8, 1884 to John Anderson and Martha Ellen Young Truman. When he was six years old, the family moved to Independence, Missouri where Harry spent his youth. He joined the Missouri National Guard and served in France during World War I. He married Elizabeth Virginia Wallace on June 29, 1919. They had one child, Mary Margaret, who became a concert soprano. Truman operated a clothing store in Kansas City that failed during an economic depression that hit in 1921. He decided to enter politics and, with the help of Tom Pendergast, local Democratic Party boss, rose from being a United States Senator to the presidency.

## Dwight D. Eisenhower, 34th President, 1952-1960:

Dwight David Eisenhower was born in Denison, Texas on October 14, 1890. At age 2, his family moved to Abilene, Kansas where he went to high school. He graduated from West Point in the same class as Omar Bradley and James Van Fleet. He became an aide to General Douglas MacArthur and helped develop the Philippine military. He was promoted to Brigadier General in 1941; and, in 1942 commanded the Allied invasion of North Africa. In 1943, he became a full general and directed the invasion of Sicily and Italy. He commanded the invasion of Normandy in 1944 bringing about Germany's surrender in 1945.

Eisenhower retired from the military and became President of Columbia University. In December 1950, he became Supreme Commander of all NATO forces. In 1952, he reluctantly agreed to become the Republican nominee for president. He campaigned against the way Truman handled the Korean War and he easily beat Adlai Stevenson of Illinois. As president, Eisenhower worked to improve the nation's welfare system and roads. His political philosophy was to give more power back to the states. An agreement was reached with Canada to build the Saint Lawrence Seaway. The U.S. took the lead in organizing 8 nations known as SEATO to resist communism in Southeast Asia. Eisenhower had a heart attack during his first term; but, he decided that his health was good enough to run for a second term. In the election of 1956, he beat Stevenson by an ever wider margin. In 1957, Eisenhower sent troops to Arkansas to enforce school integration. In July, Congress organized NASA to coordinate America's space efforts. The U.S. broke off diplomatic relations with Cuba after Premier Fidel Castro seized American property. Eisenhower suffered a stroke his second term and had several more heart attacks after he left office. He died of a heart attack in March 1969 and is buried in Abilene.

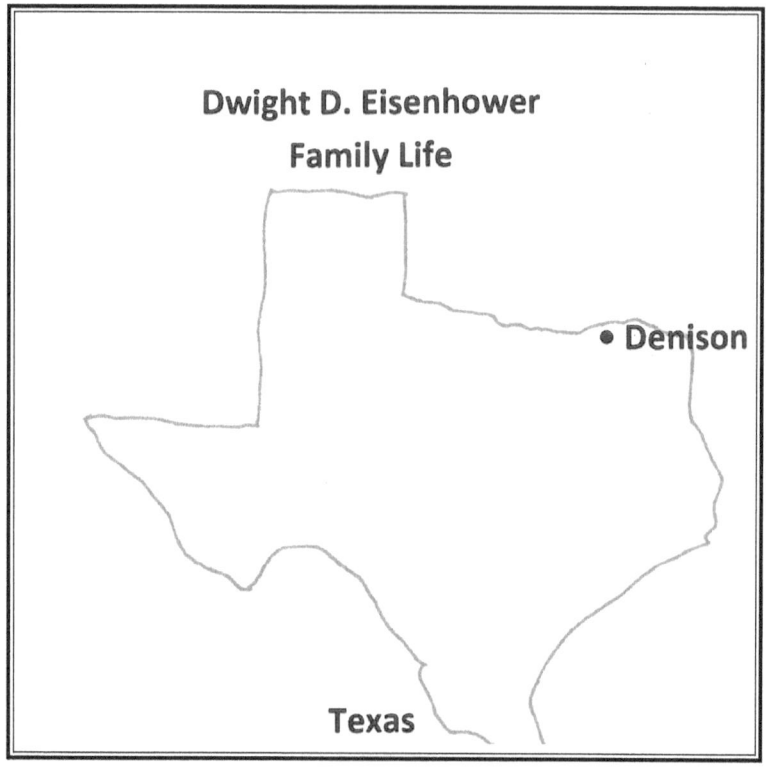

Dwight David Eisenhower was born in Denison, Texas on October 14, 1890 to David Jacob and Ida Elizabeth Stover Eisenhower. He was the third of seven children in the family. When Dwight was two, the family moved to Abilene, Kansas. The family was poor and Dwight had to work while going to school. He entered the United States Military Academy at West Point on June, 1911. He graduated in 1915 and was assigned to Fort Sam Houston in Texas. There he met Mamie Geneva Doud. They were married on July 1, 1916. They had two sons, Doud Dwight Eisenhower who died at age three, and John Shelton Doud Eisenhower who became Ambassador to Belgium in 1969. Grandson David married Julie Nixon, daughter of Vice President Richard Nixon. The various military positions that Eisenhower held brought him the fame that carried him to the White House.

**John F. Kennedy, 35th President, 1960 – 1963:** John F. Kennedy, at age 43, was the youngest man to be elected president. While in office, he enjoyed great worldwide popularity because of his youth and vigor. He was shot to death on November 22, 1963, just two years and ten months into his term of office.

Kennedy was born in Brookline, Massachusetts in 1917. He graduated from Harvard University and, during World War II, enlisted in the Navy where he captained a PT boat in the Pacific. His boat was sunk and he survived winning the Purple Heart.

He became a member of the U.S. House and Senate and, in 1960, was the Democratic nominee for president. He went on to defeat Richard Nixon by fewer than 120,000 votes. Kennedy asked Congress for legislation guaranteeing the rights of all citizens regardless of race, religion, or creed. In 1961, Cubans living in the U.S. were defeated in an attempt to take back their country from the communists. In 1962, he blockaded Cuba and turned back Russian ships carrying missiles having the range of reaching the U.S. In 1963, the U.S., Great Britain, and Russia signed a treaty banning all nuclear testing except those conducted underground.

On November 22, 1963, while riding in a motorcade through the streets of Dallas, Texas, Kennedy was shot and killed. Lee Harvey Oswald, an admitted communist was charged with the murder. Two days later, as Oswald was being led to an armored car, he was shot and killed by Jack Ruby, a Dallas tavern owner. Vice-President, Lyndon B. Johnson was sworn in the day Kennedy was killed. Kennedy was buried in Arlington National Cemetery in Virginia. Kennedy, the 35th president, and William Howard Taft, the 27th president, have been the only two presidents to be buried in Arlington National Cemetery.

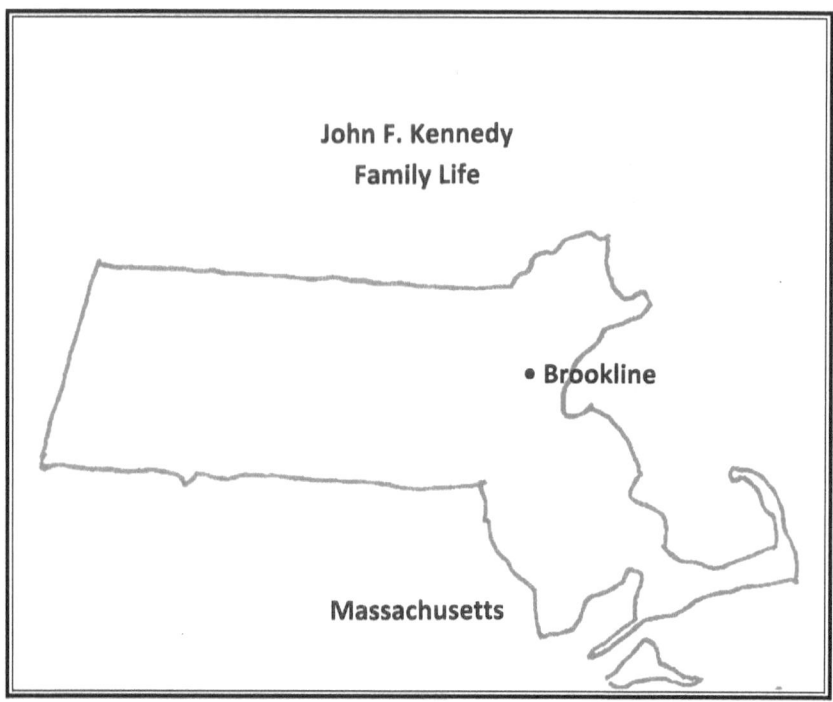

John F. Kennedy was born on May 29, 1917 in Brookline, Massachusetts to Joseph Patrick and Rose Fitzgerald Kennedy. Both of young Kennedy's parents came from families that were involved heavily in politics in the Boston area. John was the second child in a family of nine. Two of his brothers, Robert and Ted, became U.S. Senators. As he was growing up, Kennedy attended various schools including Princeton and Harvard where he graduated cum laude in 1940. After Japan attacked Pearl Harbor, young Kennedy enlisted in the Navy where he became commander of a PT boat. After a Japanese destroyer rammed his boat, Kennedy swam to a nearby island towing an injured crewman to safety. Kennedy returned to win election to the U.S. House of Representatives from Boston which started his political career to the White House..

**Lyndon B. Johnson, 36th President, 1963-1968:** Lyndon Baines Johnson was elevated to the presidency in 1963 when President John F. Kennedy was assassinated in Dallas, Texas. Johnson was elected to a full term in 1964 but refused to run again in 1968 when the violence in the Vietnam War was escalating.

Lyndon Johnson was born in Stonewall, Texas in 1908 and graduated from Southwest Texas State University. He became a member of the U.S. House but entered the Navy after Japan attacked Pearl Harbor. After World War II, he was elected to the U.S. Senate where he became Majority Leader.

In the presidential election of 1960, Democrats Kennedy and Johnson narrowly defeated Republicans Nixon and Lodge. On November 22, 1963, after serving two years and 10 months, President Kennedy was shot and killed while riding in an open limousine in Dallas, Texas. Johnson took the oath of office the same day. Johnson carried out the social policies started by former President Kennedy.

Johnson easily won the 1964 election beating Barry Goldwater of Arizona. In 1965, he sent the first combat troops to Vietnam and by 1968, there were 500,000 troops stationed there. The nation became divided over the U.S. involvement in the war and Johnson scaled down the bombing. On May 13, 1968, peace talks with North Vietnam started in Paris. At home social unrest increased and rioting broke out in some of the major U.S. cities. Johnson announced that he would not seek reelection because of the division within the country.

Johnson retired to his ranch in Texas and died after suffering two heart attacks. He was buried on his ranch in Stonewall. The Lyndon B. Johnson Library at the University of Texas Austin has many of his papers and souvenirs.

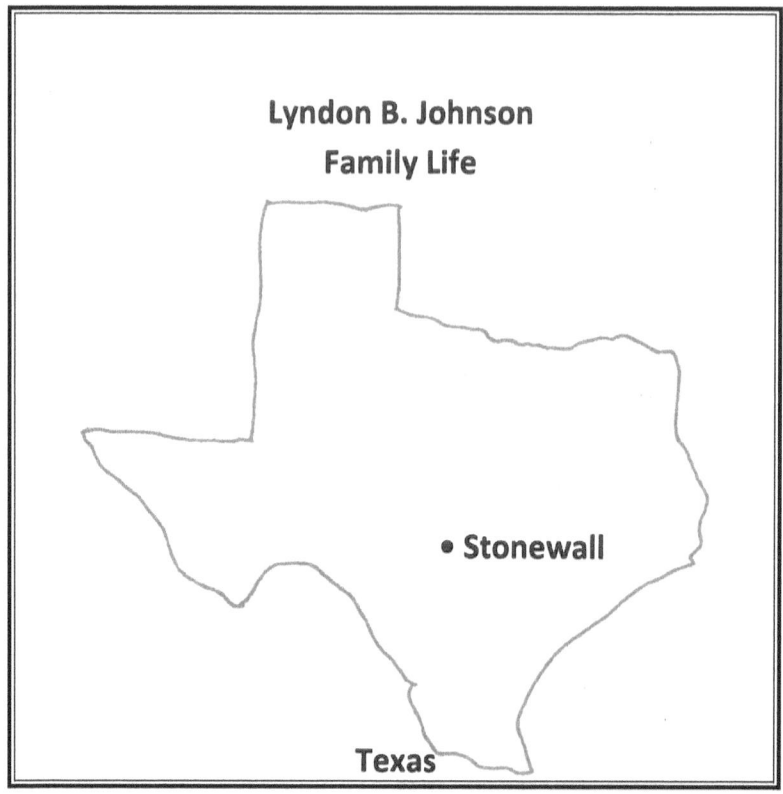

Lyndon Baines Johnson was born in Stonewall, Texas on August 27, 1908 to Samuel Ealy and Rebekah Baines Johnson. He was the eldest of five children born to Samuel and Rebekah Johnson who were school teachers. The family moved to Johnson City, Texas where Lyndon graduated from high school in 1924 at age 15. In 1927 Lyndon entered Southwest Texas State University; graduated in 1930; and became a high school teacher in Houston, Texas. In 1931, Johnson became a congressional secretary in Washington D.C. Later, while on a political meeting In Austin, Texas, he met Claudia Alta Taylor whom he married on November 17, 1934. They had two daughters, Lynda Bird and Lucy Baines. Johnson was elected to the U.S. House of Representatives in 1937. He became a follower and friend of President Roosevelt who helped him succeed in politics.

**Richard M. Nixon, 37th President, 1968-1974:** Richard Milhous Nixon was the first president to resign from office. He resigned over the threat of impeachment for the cover-up of the burglary of the Democratic Party National Headquarters. Nixon did have notable achievements such as ending the Vietnam War, reestablishing relations with China, and improving relations with Russia.

Nixon was born in 1913, in Yorba Linda, California. He graduated from Whittier College and the Duke University Law School. He served in the Navy during World War II in the Pacific. In 1946 he was elected to the U.S. House where he gained national attention for his role in convicting Alger Hiss of giving secrets to Russian agents. He was elected to the Senate in 1950 and then became Eisenhower's Vice President in 1952 and 1956. After that he suffered several defeats. In 1960, he narrowly lost the presidency to Kennedy; and, in 1962, lost the California governorship to Pat Brown. In 1964, he campaigned for Barry Goldwater who lost the presidency to Lyndon Johnson.

In the presidential election of 1968, Nixon narrowly defeated Hubert Humphrey. In 1969, he started to remove troops from Vietnam. In 1970, he formed the EPA to curtail air pollution. In 1972, he visited China and reestablished relations with a country that had been unfriendly to the U.S.. That same year, he visited Russia and reached agreement on nuclear weapon limitations. Russia also became a major buyer of U.S. grain.

Nixon easily defeated George McGovern in the election of 1972. The next year, the U.S. agreed to stop fighting in Vietnam. Nixon ended the draft and started an all voluntary Army. The Watergate scandal hit in 1973 when tapes revealed that Nixon had approved a cover-up six days after it happened. Nixon resigned on August 9, 1973 after he was faced with impeachment. Gerald Ford was sworn in the same day. On September 8, Ford pardoned Nixon in an effort to unite the country.

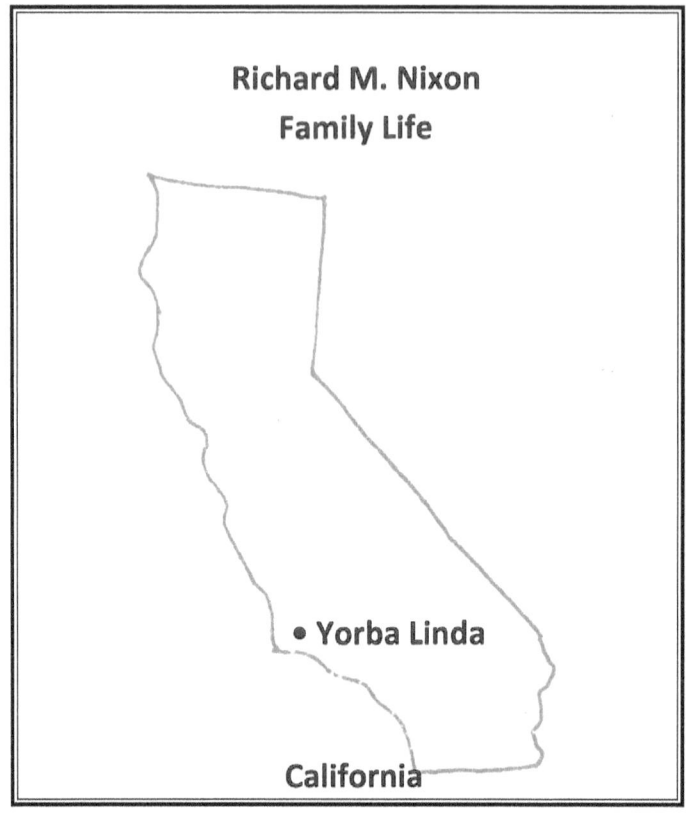

Richard Milhous Nixon was born in Yorba Linda, California on January 9, 1913 to Francis Anthony and Hannah Milhous Nixon. President Nixon had four brothers. He did odd jobs as a youth and attended Whittier High School where he excelled in debating and football. He earned a law degree from Duke University in Durham, North Carolina. Nixon returned to Whittier and married Thelma Catharine Ryan on June 21, 1940. They had two daughters, Patricia and Julie. Julie married David Eisenhower, grandson of former President Dwight Eisenhower. Nixon joined the Navy and saw duty in the Pacific in a non-combat role then retiring as a lieutenant commander. He was elected to the U.S. House of Representatives from California where he began his journey to the White House.

**Gerald B. Ford, 38th President, 1974-1976:** Gerald Ford followed Nixon to office after Nixon resigned as a result of the Watergate scandal. As president, Ford pardoned Nixon for any crimes that he committed while in office.

Gerald Ford was born in Omaha Nebraska in 1913. He was named for his father, Leslie Lynch King. His parents divorced when he was two and he and his mother moved to Grand Rapids, Michigan. She married Gerald R. Ford who adopted young Gerry and gave him his new name.

Ford was elected to the U.S. House in 1948 from Michigan. He was reelected eight times after being chosen Minority Leader.

In 1972, Nixon and Agnew easily won reelection. In 1973, federal investigators found that Agnew had accepted bribes while Governor of Maryland. He was replaced by Ford as Vice-President. After Nixon resigned, Ford was sworn in and pardoned Nixon.

Assassination attempts were made on Ford twice during his presidency. In September 1975, Lynette Fromme, follower of Charles Manson, pointed a gun at Ford and was quickly subdued. Sara Moore, a former member of a protest group, shot at Ford in San Francisco and missed. Both were sentenced to life in prison. Because of high unemployment, Ford signed legislation to create jobs and lower federal income tax.

In the presidential election of 1976, Ford narrowly lost to Jimmy Carter. In 1981, the Gerald R. Ford museum opened in Grand Rapids, Michigan along with the Ford Library in Ann Arbor, Michigan.

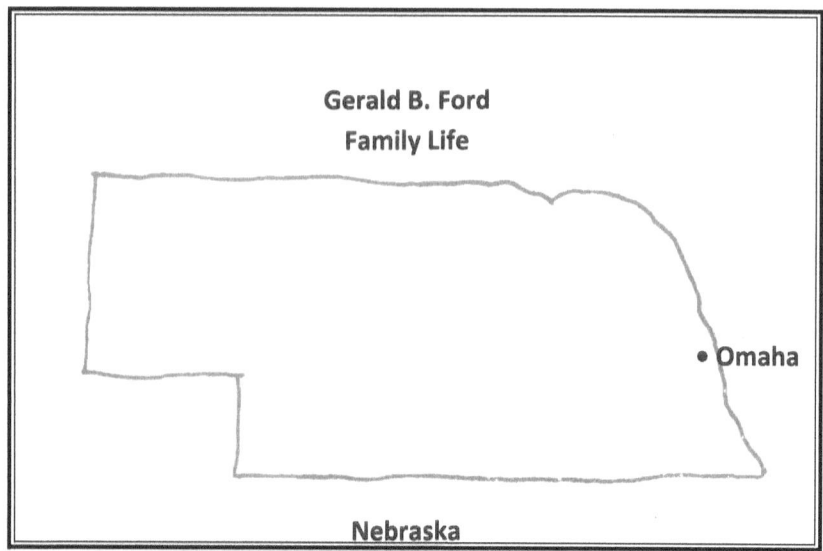

**Gerald B. Ford Family Life**

Omaha

Nebraska

Gerald Rudolph Ford was born in Omaha, Nebraska on July 14, 1913 to Leslie Lynch and Dorothy Gardner King. He was named after his father. His parents divorced when he was two years old. His mother took him to Grand Rapids, Michigan where she married Gerald Ford who adopted him and gave him his own name. Gerald had three half-brothers on his mother's side and a half brother and two half-sisters on his father's side who also remarried. Ford grew up in Grand Rapids excelling in sports and doing odd jobs. He played football for the University of Michigan graduating in 1935. He went on to receive a law degree from Yale University in 1941. He passed the Michigan bar and started a law office in Grand Rapids. When World War II started, he enlisted in the Navy and took part in naval battles in the Pacific Ocean. Back in Grand Rapids, Ford was elected to the U.S. House 13 times. He married Elizabeth Bloomer on October 15, 1948. They had four children. Ford's long standing in the House of Representatives gained him Speaker of the House and Vice-President of the United States.

**Jimmy Carter, 39th President, 1976-1980:** James Earl Carter made an impressive rise to fame from Governor of Georgia to the presidency. He was a likeable man who served with honor and resolve.

Jimmy Carter was born in 1924 in Plains, Georgia. He attended the Naval Academy and then served on battleships and submarines. He worked for Hyman Rickover in developing the world's first nuclear-powered submarine. In 1953, after the death of his father, Carter returned to Georgia to manage the family business. In 1970, he was elected Governor of Georgia.

Before the 1976 presidential primaries, Carter was little known outside Georgia. His personal appearances in all the state primary election campaigns gained him wide popularity winning him the democratic nomination. He campaigned returning just leadership to the country following Nixon's Watergate scandal. Carter and vice-presidential candidate Walter Mondale of Minnesota narrowly defeated incumbent Gerry Ford and Bob Dole of Kansas.

During Carter's first year in office the economy improved and unemployment fell. In 1978, inflation surfaced causing a major problem to Carter's popularity. That same year, the Senate ratified the treaty giving the canal to Panama. Carter received praise for his efforts in achieving a peace treaty between Egypt and Israel. When Russia invaded Afghanistan, he asked the Senate to delay ratification of the SALT arms agreement. Carter broke off relations with Iran when they overthrew the Shah and captured the U.S. Embassy. Hostages were taken and not released until the day Carter left office.

In 1980, Carter and Mondale lost the national election to Ronald Reagan and George Bush, former ambassador to the United Nations. Carter founded the Carter Center of Emory University in Atlanta, Georgia in 1982.

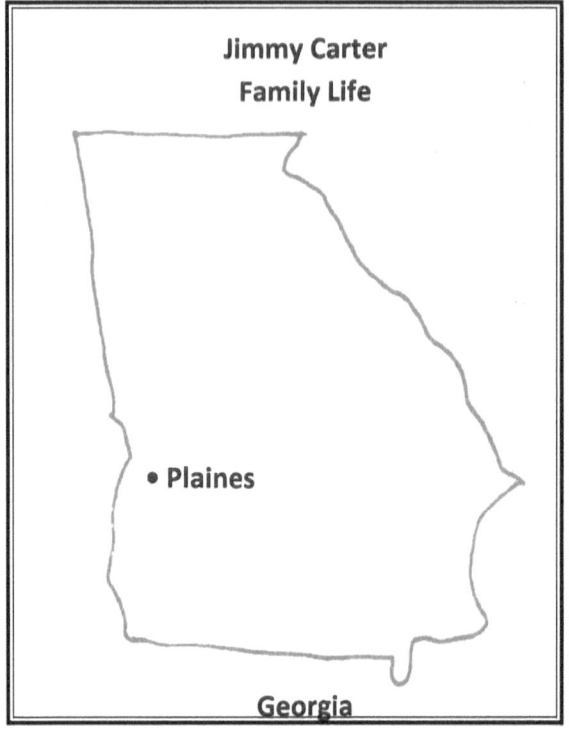

Jimmy Carter was born in Plains, Georgia on October 1, 1924 to James Earl and Bessie Lillian Gordy Carter; the first president born in a hospital. He is the eldest of four children. Carter was an excellent student and basketball player in Plains High School. He graduated high in his class at the U.S. Naval Academy with a science degree. In 1946, he married Rosalynn Smith with whom he had four children. Carter worked with Captain Hyman Rickover on the development of nuclear powered submarines. Upon his father's death, Carter resigned from the navy and made a success of the family peanut farm. He held various political positions in Georgia; and, in 1971, was elected governor. Being elected governor of Georgia gave him enough of the national attention he needed to run for president.

**Ronald Reagan, 40th President, 1980-1988:** Ronald Reagan lived a storied life. He was an athletic, a radio broadcaster, a movie actor, a governor, and the president. At age 69, Ronald Reagan was the oldest man to be elected president. He was one of four former presidents to reach the age of 90; and, is one of a few presidents to change political parties. One of Reagan's greatest achievements was contributing to the fall of the Soviet Empire.

Ronald Reagan was born in Tampico, Illinois in 1911. He graduated from Eureka College, Eureka, Illinois, after which he became a radio broadcaster. In 1937, he moved to California and became a movie actor; first in films and later on TV

In 1962, Reagan switched to the Republican Party. He was elected Governor of California in 1966 and 1970. He lost the 1976 presidential nomination to Gerald Ford who, in turn, lost the election to Jimmy Carter. In 1980, Reagan beat Carter. As Reagan was giving his inaugural address, 52 U.S. hostages were set free by Iran. In 1981, Reagan was shot by John Hinckley in Washington. Although close to death, he survived. In 1981, Reagan fired 11,345 air traffic controllers for going on an unauthorized strike. He believed in supply-side economics where, by lowering taxes, businesses would grow and people would be able to afford to buy more goods. In 1983, Reagan ordered the invasion of Granada and defeated a newly elected communist government there. Reagan called The Soviet Union "the evil empire"; but, when Mikhail Gorbachev became premier, relations between the two countries cooled and the U.S.S.R. was dissolved.

At age 83, Reagan contacted Alzheimer's disease and died 10 years later in California. His was interred in the Ronald Reagan Presidential Library in Simi Valley California.

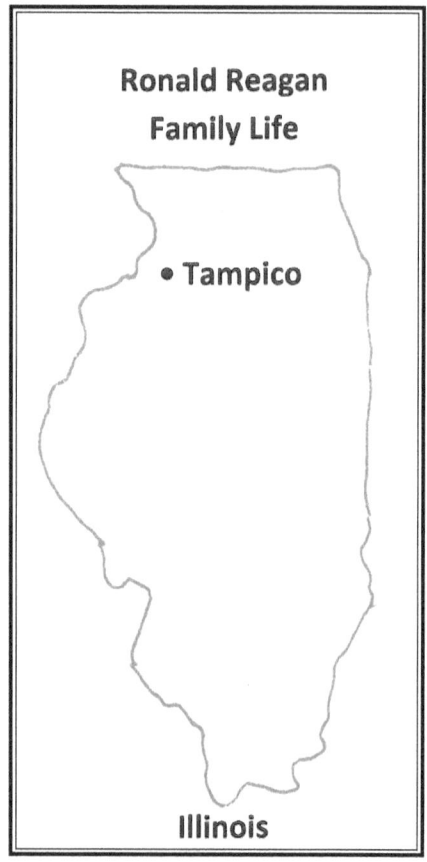

**Ronald Reagan
Family Life**

● **Tampico**

**Illinois**

Ronald Reagan was born in Tampico, Illinois on February 6, 1911, to Jack and Nellie Wilson Reagan. Reagan had one older brother in his family, Neil. In 1920, the family moved to Dixon, Illinois where Reagan attended school. He graduated from Eureka College in 1932. He traveled to Iowa where he embarked on a radio sports broadcasting career. While in California on assignment, he became a movie actor. Reagan married Jane Wyman on January 26, 1940 after starring in a movie with her. They had two children, Maureen and Christine of their own and adopted Michael. They divorced and Reagan married Nancy Davis in 1952. They had two children, Paul and Ron. Reagan became a two time governor of California leading him to the White House.

**George H.W. Bush, 41st President, 1988-1992:** George Herbert Walker Bush served many roles in government before being elected president. He was a congressman, an ambassador, Director of the Central Intelligence Agency, and Vice-President. His son, George W. Bush would become the 43rd president of the U.S.; only the second time a son of a president would take the high office.

Bush was born in Milton, Massachusetts and enlisted in the Navy at age 18, becoming an aviator throughout World War II. He graduated from Yale University in 1948 and moved to Texas where he worked his way up in the oil industry. There he was elected to the U.S. House and ran unsuccessfully for president in 1980. He was chosen by Ronald Reagan to be his running mate. They were elected beating Jimmy Carter and Walter Mondale. During tenure as vice-president, Bush headed task forces on deregulation and drugs.

In 1988, Bush ran for president and beat Democrat Michael Dukakis. He had to deal with a Democratic Congress over the problem of a high government deficit. After stating that he would not raise taxes, Bush was forced by the democrats to sign a bill that raised taxes. Bush sent 2000 troops to Panama to dethrone Manuel Noriega who had become an enemy of the U.S. He met with Soviet Mikhail Gorbachev and reached an agreement to reduce nuclear weapons by 35%. Bush initiated the "Gulf War" that drove Iraq's Saddam Hussein out of oil rich Kuwait. He started negotiations on The North American Free Trade Agreement that would later be signed by President Clinton.

Bush lost the 1992 presidential election to Bill Clinton as Clinton received 43% of the popular vote to 38% for Bush. Ross Perot received 19% of the popular vote as a third party candidate. Bush and his wife Barbara reside in Texas.

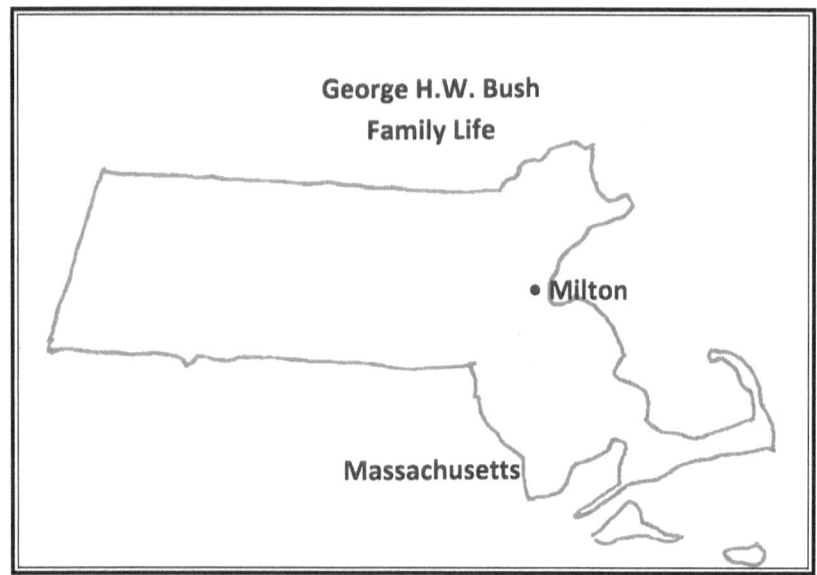

George H.W. Bush was born on June 12, 1924 in Milton, Massachusetts to Senator Prescott Sheldon and Dorothy Walker Bush. He attended Phillips Academy in Andover Massachusetts where he held many leadership roles. Bush enlisted in the Navy on his 18th birthday and became a pilot. He saw extensive action in the Pacific during World War II receiving several medals for heroism in action. Bush was honorably discharged in 1945 and married Barbara Pierce on January 6, only three weeks after returning from service in the Pacific. They had six children: George Walker, Pauline Robinson, John Ellis, Neil Mallon, Marvin Pierce, and Dorothy. He enrolled at Yale University becoming active in many student activities including being team captain of the baseball team playing in the first college world series. Bush graduated from Yale in 1948 with a Bachelor of Arts degree in economics. He moved to Texas where he became very successful in the oil exploration business. Bush was a member of the U.S. House of Representatives, Ambassador to the U.N., Chairman of the Republican Party; positions that lead him to the White House.

## William Jefferson Clinton, 42nd President, 1992-2000:

Bill Clinton took office after the Cold War ended. He is a Democrat but some of his policies are described as being "centrist". He was the third president to be tried for impeachment and the second president to be impeached. He was acquitted by the Senate.

Clinton was born in Hope, Arkansas. He graduated from Georgetown University earning a Rhodes scholarship. He received a law degree from Yale University where he met his wife, Hillary Rodham. Clinton served as Governor of Arkansas and Chairman of the National Governors Association.

Clinton won the presidency in 1992 beating incumbent George H.W. Bush. He signed the North American Free Trade Agreement but failed in an effort to pass health care reform. He approved a Department of Defense edict called "don't ask, don't tell" which allowed gay men and women to serve in the armed services without their sexuality being disclosed.

He won a second term in office, the first Democrat to do so since Franklin Delano Roosevelt in 1936. He passed welfare reform but it was in his second term that he was impeached. He was impeached for perjury and obstruction of justice for his involvement with a White House intern. He was later acquitted by the Senate. Clinton authorized the use of American forces in the NATO bombing of Yugoslavia. There were reports of Albanians being attacked by Serbs in the province of Kosovo. There was a budget surplus the last three years of Clinton's presidency. After leaving office, he received the highest approval rating of any president since World War II. The Clinton Presidential Center was opened in Little Rock, Arkansas after his last term in office. He campaigned for his wife's senate seat and her presidential nomination in 2008 and also Barack Obama's presidential campaigns of 2008 and 2012.

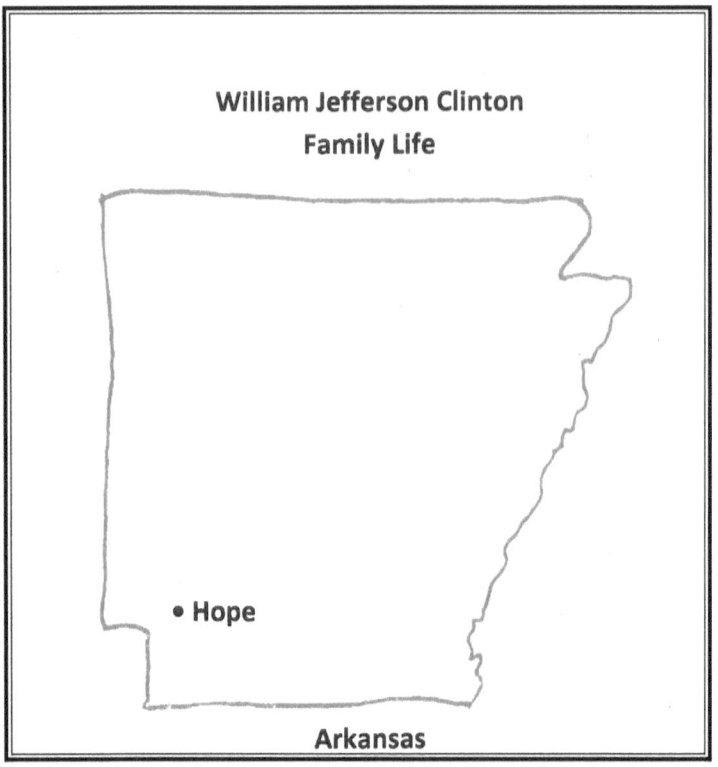

Bill Clinton was born on August 19, 1946 as William Jefferson Blythe in Hope Arkansas to William Jefferson and Virginia Dell Cassidy Blythe. Bill's father died in an automobile accident before he was born and his mother married Roger Clinton from whom Bill received his present last name. They moved to Hot Springs, Arkansas where Bill attended school. He graduated from Georgetown University and received a scholarship to attend University College, Oxford, England. Clinton received a law degree from Yale where he met Hillary. They were married on October 11, 1975 and had one child, Chelsea. Clinton became Governor of Arkansas and gained national attention when he gave the Democratic response to President Reagan's 1985 State of the Union Address.

**George W. Bush, 43rd President, 2000-2008:** George W. Bush, the eldest son of George H.W. Bush the 41st president, is the second son of a president to be elected to the high office. Previously, John Quincy Adams, the sixth president and eldest son of John Adams the second president, was the first father and son combination to ascend to the high office.

George W. was born in New Haven, Connecticut where his grandfather Prescott Bush was a U.S. Senator. He grew up in Texas and then graduated from Yale and the Harvard Business School. Bush was Governor of Texas before being elected president. His younger brother Jeb was Governor of Florida.

Bush beat Democrat Al Gore in a close election for his first term. The election went to the U.S. Supreme Court which settled a controversy over the Florida vote giving Bush the presidency. Bush had 271 electoral votes to Gore's 266.

The 9/11/01 terrorist attack on the New York Trade Center Buildings occurred nine months into Bush's presidency. He announced a war on terror and sent troops to Afghanistan and Iraq. He enacted broad tax reductions and ruled against the Kyoto Protocol global warming accords.

Bush beat Democrat John Kerry in a close election his second term. The Democrats won control of Congress in the 2006 elections. In late 2007, the U.S. entered into the longest recession since World War II. Bush received enormous popularity after winning the war in Iraq but lost favor afterwards because of the downturn in the economy.

After his term in office, Bush returned to Texas and purchased a home in the Dallas area where he has made appearances at various events. He has published his memoirs "Decision Points", where he considers his biggest accomplishments keeping America safe while his greatest failure was not being able to reform Social Security.

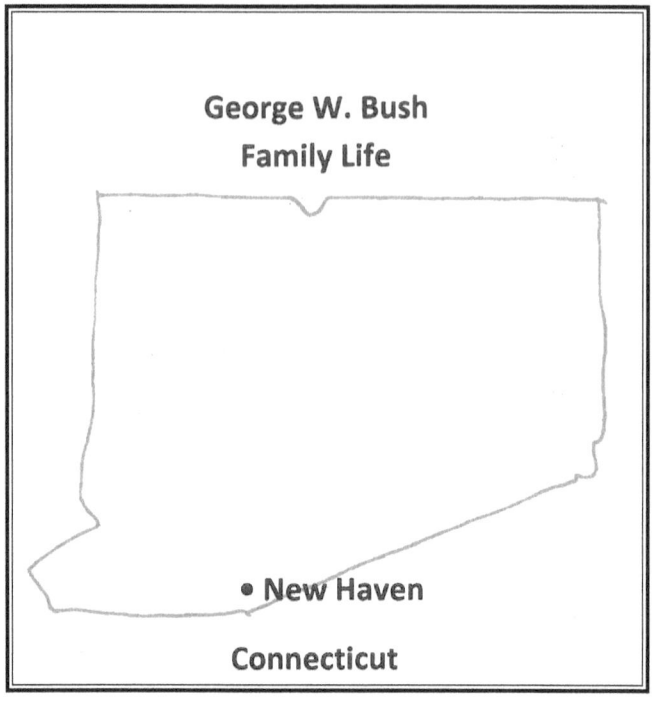

George W. Bush was born on July 6, 1946 in New Haven, Connecticut to former President George H.W. and Barbara Pierce Bush. The Bush family consisted of George, Jeb, Neil, Marvin, Dorothy, and Robin who died at an early age. The family moved to Midland and then Houston, Texas. George attended school in Midland, Houston and then Andover, Massachusetts. He studied history at Yale University where he was heavy engaged in school activities graduating with a degree in history. In 1973, he attended Harvard University receiving a Master's Degree in Business Administration; the only president to have received a Master's Degree. Bush entered the Texas Air National Guard in 1968 and was discharged in 1974, serving in Texas and Alabama. Bush married Laura Welch, a librarian on November 5, 1977. They settled in Midland, Texas where they raised twins Jenna and Barbara. Bush entered the oil business in Texas and purchased an interest in the Texas Rangers baseball team. Bush was elected Governor of Texas in 1994 and beat Al Gore for the U.S. Presidency in 2000.

**Barack Hussein Obama, 44th President, 2008-2016:** Barack Obama is the first African-American to be elected to the office of the presidency. He served when the country was in an economic downturn and heavily in debt. He signed legislation to stimulate the economy and reform health care.

Barack was born in Honolulu, Hawaii in 1961. His mother was originally from Kansas and his father from Kenya. They met while attending the University Of Hawaii. Obama graduated from Columbia University and Harvard Law School. He taught at the University of Chicago Law School. He ran unsuccessfully for the U.S. House in 2000, but came back to win a Senate seat in 2004.

He won the Democratic nomination for president beating Hillary Rodham Clinton and went on to win the presidency from Republican John McCain in the election of 2008. He was named the 2009 Nobel Peace Prize laureate. He signed legislation to create jobs and provide for unemployment benefits. He ended U.S. military involvement in Iraq and increased the number of troops in Afghanistan. He ordered the secret operation that resulted in the death of long time terrorist leader Osama bin Laden. He became the first U.S. president to support same-sex marriage.

Obama won the election for a second term in 2012 beating Republican Mitt Romney. He promised to do what is necessary to promote job growth, provide for a fair federal tax program, and to campaign to end the spread of terrorism in the world.

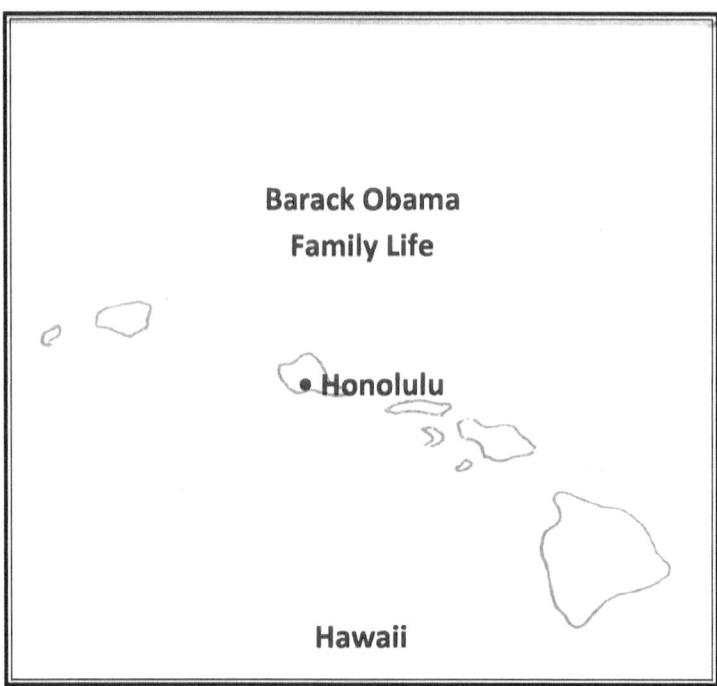

Barack Obama was born in Honolulu, Hawaii on August 4, 1961 to Stanley Ann Dunham and Barack Obama Sr. His mother was from Wichita, Kansas and father from Kenya. Obama's parents divorced and he and his mother moved to Seattle, Washington. His father returned to Kenya where he remarried, and died in 1982 in an automobile accident. His mother died in 1995 of cancer. Obama received a Bachelor of Arts degree from Columbia in 1983 and a degree from the Harvard Law School in 1991, graduating magna cum laude. He worked in Chicago as a community organizer where he met Michelle Robinson and married her in 1992. They have two daughters, Malia Ann and Natasha. He taught at the University of Chicago for twelve years and practiced as a civil rights attorney before becoming a Chicago State Senator, a U.S. Senator, and then president.

# About the Author

The author is a licensed Professional Engineer who has taken an interest in the history of the United States Presidents and political parties. Since the author is not a political scholar, this book is more of an "average citizen" approach to the subject matter as opposed to what might be written by political historians.

www.ingramcontent.com/pod-product-compliance
Lightning Source LLC
Chambersburg PA
CBHW020538290526
45786CB00002B/938